UP-TO-DATE OBJECT LESSONS

With Prayers and Scriptures

UP-TO-DATE OBJECT LESSONS

With Prayers and Scriptures

by

John H. Sargent

BAKER BOOK HOUSE
Grand Rapids, Michigan

ISBN: 0-8010-7993-4

Copyright, 1945, by
Baker Book House Company

Previously published as
66 More Modern Parables for Young Folks

PHOTOLITHOPRINTED BY CUSHING - MALLOY, INC.
ANN ARBOR, MICHIGAN, UNITED STATES OF AMERICA
1976

CONTENTS
INDEX OF PARABLE TEACHINGS

Appreciation	1	Prayer—Worship	34
	51		5
Character Building	48		39
	43		54
	30		25
	42		33
	20	Repentance	21
	66		
	4	Spiritual Power, Growth and Guidance	28
	49		37
	12		63
	55		13
Cooperation	11		45
	57		52
	24		47
	53		27
	3		41
	4		
	35	Self-control	50
	56		9
Courage	22		32
Friendliness	10		8
	14	Service, Joy of	15
	62		38
	36		46
Justice, Tolerance	29		64
	2		61
	7		18
Loyalty	65		6
	16		
	17	Trustworthiness	19
Patience	58		23
	59		26
	60		40
			31

CONTENTS

Alphabetically Arranged

Parable	Teaching	Number	Page
Anvils	Character Building	48	95
Antitoxin	Cooperation	11	21
Bridges	Spiritual Guidance and Power	28	55
Bells	Prayer and Worship	34	67
Bent Trees	Spiritual Care	37	73
Bottle, Filling a	Character Building	43	85
Bridles	Self Control	50	99
Burning Coal	Cooperation	56	111
Bridges	Cooperation	57	113
Bells Ring	Prayer	5	9
Colors	Friendliness	10	19
Cabbages	Character Building	30	59
Clock Had Stopped	Prayer	39	77
Candles	Spiritual Guidance	52	103
Coins	Loyalty	65	129
Dollar Signs	Trustworthiness	19	37
Doorways	Joy of Service	46	91
Drills	Prayer	54	107
Doorknobs	Cooperation	24	47
Envelopes	Friendliness	14	27
Electric Light Bulb	Christian Service	15	29
Fighting Shadows	Self Control	9	17
Full Measure	Justice	29	57
Focus, Correct	Cooperation	53	105
Gold, Frankincense, Myrrh	Appreciation	51	101
Grain, A Bag of	Service	38	75
Glass House	Friendliness	62	123
Hinges	Trustworthiness	23	45
Icebergs	Character Building	42	83
Insulators	Loyal Service	64	127
Keys	Self Control	32	63

Parable	Teaching	Number	Page
Leaves	*Cooperation*	3	5
Leaf, A	*Justice, Tolerance*	2	3
Leaves of a Book	*Loyalty*	16	31
Leash, A	*Spiritual Guidance*	47	93
Light, Color of	*Tolerance*	7	13
Magnetic Power	*Spiritual Power*	13	25
Models	*Trustworthiness*	26	51
Masks	*Trustworthiness*	40	79
Nails in Trees	*Character Building*	20	39
Puzzles	*Cooperation*	4	7
Pendulums	*Loyalty*	17	33
Pictures	*Spiritual Guidance*	27	153
Pail of Water	*Trustworthiness*	31	61
Picture Frames	*Character*	66	131
Roosters Crow, When	*Appreciation*	1	1
Ropes	*Cooperation*	35	69
Roots Shape Trees	*Character Building*	44	87
Roads—Hairpin Turns	*Patience*	58	115
Roads—Switchback	*Patience*	59	117
Roads—Pigtail	*Patience*	60	119
Steak	*Joy of Service*	6	11
Smudges	*Repentance*	21	41
Steeples	*Prayer, Worship*	25	49
Stencils	*Friendliness, Loyalty*	36	71
Swimming, Straight	*Spiritual Guidance*	41	81
Stairways	*Spiritual Growth*	45	89
Snowball, Color of	*Character Building*	49	97
Salt	*Christian Service*	61	121
Typewriter Keys	*Self Control*	8	15
Tone	*Character Building*	12	23
Three Shingles	*Service*	18	35
Thermostat	*Prayer*	33	65
Tire Treads	*Character Building*	55	109
Thermometers	*Spiritual Care*	63	125
Weather Vane	*Courage*	22	43

I

WHEN ROOSTERS CROW

One of the most interesting and queer looking, yet beautiful of birds, is the rooster. I suppose he got his funny name because he sits on a roost, or perch, when he sleeps.—(Or did the roost get its name from the rooster?) (It's like,—which came first the hen or the egg?)

Did you ever see a rooster crow?

Did you ever see a rooster crow without looking up?

Did you ever see a rooster?

When roosters crow we may be sure they have found something to crow about—such as a " New Day." Even before the sun comes up he jumps onto a fence top, flaps his wings and stretches his neck and looks up and crows.

It may be he has scratched up a new bright colored worm, a kind he has never seen before. He is proud of his flock so he crows about his home. He sees things, indeed he scratches around to find things, and lifts his head as though to thank God. Indeed the rooster never crows without lifting his head.

When I talk with some men and hear them complain about the Government; about overwork; about taxes, and talk about money as though it made peace and world democracy—I like to think of the rooster and wonder why, instead of grumbling, we all don't try harder to find things to look up and crow about!

Perhaps IF we looked up oftener we would crow. Let us be thankful for God, for prayer, for opportunities to worship, for churches,—thankful enough to lift up our heads and hearts towards God for giving us the opportunity to have a part in making a better world by cheering, and working for Him and for mankind.

" *Lift up your heads O ye gates and be ye lifted up ye everlasting doors and the King of Glory shall come in.*"— Psalm 24: 7.

A PRAYER

"Our Father who art in heaven."

We thank Thee, dear God, that Thou art our Father, for a father loves his children and cares for them, and we are Thy children.

Thy Son Jesus has taught us that we are Thine, and that Thy love for us is very great—even as great as our parents', and greater.

So we are thankful because Thou hast given us so much to enjoy. We thank Thee for the pets we have—the bird, the kitten, our dog. We thank Thee for health and strength to enjoy our play.

Every new day there is something different to enjoy, for which we may give thanks and share with friends. Accept our appreciation each day, dear Lord. Amen.

A Message from Our Bible

"The earth is the Lord's and the fulness thereof; the world, and they that dwell therein.

For he hath founded it upon the seas, and established it upon the floods.

Who shall ascend into the hill of the Lord? or who shall stand in his holy place?

He that hath clean hands and a pure heart;

He shall receive the blessing from the Lord . . .

Lift up your heads O ye gates; and be ye lifted up ye everlasting doors; and the King of glory shall come in.

Who is the King of glory? The Lord strong and mighty—he is the King of glory."—Psalm 24.

A LEAF

The other day I was admiring a small plant on the table by the window and I started to count the leaves. There were just ten. Every leaf was different from any other leaf on the plant. So I looked at another plant and counted its leaves. Of the twenty-six leaves there were no two exactly alike!

Try counting the leaves on the tree that grows near the window of your house and then go out and see if, among these thousands, you can find two exactly alike—my guess is that out of the billions and trillions of leaves in your state there won't be found two alike.

We often speak of "identical twins" but even though they look alike we know there is a difference somewhere—if only in their fingerprints. Their ideas and ideals are different—one becomes a preacher and the other an electrical engineer.

Everything God made—a leaf—a spear of grass—an ant—you—is an individual creation on His part. That makes you pretty important in His sight. But you must remember that the person next you is just as important—whether he is white or black or brown.

"*He shall be like a tree—his leaf also shall not wither.*"—(*Read* PSALM 1 : 3.)

A PRAYER

"Our Father who art in heaven, hallowed be Thy name." Teach us to pray, as Jesus did, not selfishly, but thinking first of others, that we may be helpful in making Thy love live in our midst.

We see Thy love expressed in the beauty of growing things,—of trees and plants, that we enjoy so much, and in seeing these we honor Thy great power which can do what we can never accomplish.

As Jesus did His best, let us also be faithful in our praise of Thy name, and so live as to give joy to all around us.

Keep us faithful to Christ's way. Amen.

A Message from Our Bible

" Blessed is the man that walketh not in the counsel of the ungodly, nor standeth in the way of sinners, nor sitteth in the seat of the scornful.

But his delight is in the law of the Lord; and in his law doth he meditate day and night.

And he shall be like a tree planted by the rivers of water, that bringeth forth his fruit in his season; his leaf also shall not wither and whatsoever he doeth shall prosper.

The Lord knoweth the way of the righteous."—From Psalm i.

3
LEAVES

In my parable about a leaf I suggested to you how important God considers us and all things He has made—I wonder if you counted the leaves on that tree growing by your house. How many did you find just alike?

When there is only one leaf on a tree it is a pretty sure sign that tree is nearly dead. At least the value of it is greatly limited—indeed very small. And so it is cut down for firewood.

Not only is a tree healthy when it shows many leaves but a whole community is much more healthy when there are a lot of trees and leaves. It is said in the New Testament that on the tree of life by the pure water are "—leaves of the tree for the healing of the nations." That's right! Leaves take in (eat) much of the poison in the air and give out gallons of water into the atmosphere surrounding them.

So all these trillions of leaves on trees co-operate towards making a healthier world.

Well, the Church can heal the nation too if all its friends will work together and stick to their job of giving Christianity.

The leaves teach us so well that we are valuable as individuals, only as we work together.

"In the midst of the street of it, and on either side of the river, was there the tree of life, which bare twelve manner of fruits, and yielded her fruit every month: and the leaves of the tree were for the healing of the nation."
—Revelation 22:2.

A PRAYER

"Thy kingdom come."

Dear Jesus, use us in Thy plan for a Christian world. We would be Thy helpers through our home and church in making Thy kingdom an example for us here in our community.

Speak to our hearts as young folks, that we may know just what is best and what is right for us.

Please help us to make peace in the world, and so bring safety and health to all people and all nations. As Thy kingdom is built upon love and peace, direct our thoughts that we may grow, as Jesus did, not only in stature, but also in the love of God. Teach us each day how to be helpful, in Thy service. Amen.

A Message from Our Bible

"And he shewed me a pure river of water of life, clear as crystal, proceeding out of the throne of God . . .

In the midst of the street and on either side of the river there was a tree of life—and the leaves of the tree were for the healing of the nations."—Rev. 22.

"Save me O God by thy name, and judge me by thy strength. Hear my prayer, O God; give ear to the words of my mouth. Behold God is mine helper; the Lord is with them that uphold my soul."—Psalm 54.

4
PUZZLES

Some years ago it seemed that everyone was "doing" those picture jig saw puzzles. Each one of those two hundred pieces had to be in its right place. It wouldn't fit anywhere else or make a good picture if forced to be anywhere but in its own place.

Oftentimes a thread of color drawn through the picture gives it its beauty—and if one piece is in wrong, that color scheme is broken!

I used to have a puzzle of the United States—each state was cut out. Now, some of those western states are almost square, so that one might put Wyoming where New Mexico should be!—but the map of the United States isn't quite right with New Mexico north of Colorado—even though it might still bring four states to border each other so that a man can actually sit in four states at the same time!

Then I also recall how our cat chewed up Montana! This of course left it badly broken and soiled, so that the completed map or picture was no longer beautiful.

I've seen people like "New Mexico," butting in and trying to take credit that rightfully belongs to some other boy or girl.

I'm sure that, as Americans and workers in the church, we won't ever let bad habits and selfish ways cause us to leave any empty places or jagged spots in our Christian organization—for each of us must fill the place acceptably, and do the work he can do as God desires of him, that the world tomorrow may be as He planned it through co-operation in unselfish service.

"*We are one in Christ and every one members one of another.*"—Romans 12:5.

A PRAYER

"Thy will be done on earth as in heaven."

Dear Jesus, bless this home, and let us never forget to thank Thee for teaching us how to pray.

Give each one of us strength and a will to do our work as Thou would have it done; and in our play make us "be fair" and unselfish, and good losers.

In that way we fit into our place with others in helping make Thy will real on earth, through Thy teachings, O Lord. Amen.

A Message from Our Bible

"For as we have many members in one body, and all members have not the same office;

So we being many are one in Christ and every one members one of another.

Having gifts differing according to the grace that is given to us whether prophecy, let us prophesy according to the proportion of faith;

Or ministry, let us wait on our ministering; or he that teacheth, on teaching.

Be kindly affectioned one to another with brotherly love; in honour preferring one another.

Not slothful in business; fervent in spirit; serving the Lord;

Rejoicing in hope; patient in tribulation; continuing instant in prayer."—Romans 12.

5
WHEN BELLS RING

I HAVE a string of bells hanging in the study of my home. They remind me of the days when I used to drive horses and enjoy the jingling of the sleigh bells as the horse speeded over the slippery roads.

As I walk by those bells sometimes I reach out and touch them, and every one of those forty-one tiny globes on that strap start to ring. So it occurred to me that our church bell rings each Sunday calling people's attention to the church service for worship. But particularly, I thought, that bell rings because someone sets it in motion.

On the sea just off shore near some rock, is a buoy with a bell on it. It rings out its warning to sailors because the movement of the waves sets it in motion.

When your telephone bell rings you rush to answer the call before the person hangs up. Why does that bell ring? Or the doorbell?

Well, first, because someone wants to talk with you; and second, and this is the actual reason it rings, that person set the bell in motion.

We all want to talk with God and get His advice and help. We can, you know, anytime,—but WE must act; WE must pull the rope and set in motion bells of our faith and trust, and talk to Him and then wait for His answer. That is prayer.

"*He went up into a mountain apart to pray, and was alone.*"—MATTHEW 14:23.

A PRAYER

"Give us this day our daily bread."

Dear Lord, help them who watch over us and our home, that they may not worry because of sickness or hardship.

Give us a desire to do our part in making this a happy place and a peaceful world. We know our prayers will be answered IF we pray, so let us never forget to talk to Thee, for in doing so we show our love, and our faith in Thee.

Hear our prayers, O God, and lead us in Thy truth. Amen.

A Message from Our Bible

"And Jesus went forth, and saw a great multitude, and was moved with compassion toward them, and he healed their sick.

And he commanded the multitude to sit down on the grass and took the five loaves and two fishes and looking up to heaven, he blessed and brake and gave the loaves to the disciples and the disciples to the multitude.

And they did all eat and were filled; and they took up of the fragments that remained twelve baskets full.

And they that had eaten were about five thousand men, beside women and children.

And when he had sent the multitude away, he went up into a mountain apart to pray."—Matthew 14.

6
A PIECE OF STEAK

We were enjoying a steak dinner at our house some time ago and at the end of the meal there was a small piece of that delicious meat left on the platter. I expect Mrs. Sargent was planning how it would be used for supper or tomorrow's dinner when Bob spoke up and asked if he could give it to Queenie. Queenie is a neighbor's dog and we have permission to give her a bone or a piece of meat at any time.

When Bob asked to give that piece of steak to Queenie he was immediately denied the privilege. "Surely you know that steak is scarce." "We can't afford to waste points on a dog." "Anyway we will use it tomorrow." Then to console Bob one of us said, "You know, if Queenie doesn't taste the meat she won't know what she has missed."

"I know *she* won't know what she has missed," said Bob, "but I will."

I think that is why we give Christmas presents and share our Thanksgiving dinner sometimes because we enjoy seeing others happy when we are. That's why Dr. Grenfell went to Labrador. That's why Livingstone went to Africa to give the things they enjoyed.

There are a great many boys and girls right here in our state and in our country who do not know who Jesus Christ was and what Christianity is and what it means to our lives. I'm sure you want them to "taste" that contentment which you enjoy so much every day.

"*O taste and see that the Lord is good.*"—Psalm 34:8.

A PRAYER

"Forgive us our debts as we forgive our debtors."

Dear God, put into our minds the forgiving spirit.

We dislike to be angry, so teach us to overcome such feelings when they come to us. If others seem to hurt us let us remember that we may be partly at fault.

Help us to be generous with our friendliness and so teach others the way of Christian consideration.

Bless our church, because by it Thy love is conveyed to people throughout the whole world, and there are opportunities for all to serve Thee in Christ's name. Amen.

A Message from Our Bible

"O taste and see that the Lord is good; blessed is the man that trusteth in him.

Come, ye children, hearken unto me; I will teach you the fear of the Lord.

Keep thy tongue from evil, and thy lips from speaking guile.

Depart from evil, and do good; seek peace, and pursue it.

The eyes of the Lord are upon the righteous, and his ears are open unto their cry."—Psalm 34.

7
THE COLOR OF LIGHT

We all take light for granted as a part of everyday life. It is given to us, either naturally or artificially, and we use it without thinking much about its color, or even saying "thank you." It's enough for us that we can see by light.

When there is no light we say it is dark; therefore darkness must be black.—Light, being the opposite of dark, must then be white! But light doesn't look like the color of snow or white paint!

Did you ever see a beautiful sunrise? The whole atmosphere of the morning light seemed ablaze with color.

The colorful leaves of fall give a red tint to a whole community.

When is it that you see the colorful rainbow? When you see light through raindrops.

Whatever color light is, to us, seems to depend upon what is between us and the source of that light. If, at night, the light of a room is red, it is because of red bulbs.

A boy or girl who has lived all his life in Honolulu, and his father and mother were born there, probably has a brown skin but we as Christians, and surely God, see beyond and deeper than the color of the outside—we see through this and see a heart and mind just like ours.

So the color of light, as we see it, isn't very important, —or of a person. When you look at a box of chocolates through a showcase, don't think it is purple just because it looks that way—it may be the showcase glass is purple! Or when a person looks black—remember HE is just like you, only his skin is black!

"*For God has made of one blood all nations of the earth.*"—Acts 17:26.

A PRAYER

"Lead us not into temptation."

Our Father in heaven, teach all Thy children the right, when they have to decide between doing one thing or another.

Let the power of Thy love be so strong within all, that temptations will be overcome. Thou, O God, will lead all people to do Thy will, if only they themselves will follow the instructions of Jesus; and so temptations fade away.

In prayer, young folks may talk to Thee, and Thou wilt answer, so that the inner feelings of all will be led by the light of Thy guiding love. Hear our prayer, O God, that we may be directed aright through Jesus' way of enlightenment. Amen.

A Message from Our Bible

" God who made the world and all things therein, seeing that he is Lord of heaven and earth, dwelleth not in houses made with hands; neither is worshipped with men's hands, as though he needed any thing, seeing he giveth to all life, and breath, and all things;

And hath made of one blood all nations of men . . .

That they should seek the Lord if haply they might feel after him, and find him, though he be not far from every one of us;

But in him we live, and move, and have our being,— for we are also his children.

Forasmuch then as we are the children of God, we ought not to think that he is like unto gold, or silver, or stone, graven by art and man's device.

He will judge the world in righteousness by Jesus whom he hath ordained; whereof he hath given assurance unto all."—From the 17th Chapter of The Acts.

TYPEWRITER KEYS

A TYPEWRITER is like a piano in many respects; you have to learn where each key is located on the machine, and the letters they represent. You not only have to learn the twenty-six letters and the nine of ten numbers, and a few punctuation marks—but you have to learn how to hit them.

Merely to know where the keys are is not quite enough. A good stenographer hits the right key at the right time in the right place and rapidly!

When you are sick the doctor comes and tells you what pills to take and when to take them, and if you trust his advice and follow his instructions you get well faster.

All of you have faith in God and know what He wants you to do, but sometimes boys and girls are like the following typewritten line: 697 ih930 3h457 6y3 i36w q43 h85 708 eOn85 u85 5y3 49ty5 Oj3w—you know where the keys are but you don't hit the right ones —— It just doesn't make sense to know something to be true but act as though it were not. Whatever key you hit that letter is recorded.

Every Sunday you go to Sunday school and to church and you learn what is right. It's up to you to hit those " right " keys when you are at home or at school or out in the ball park for there is where your character will show you up as to the kind of boy or girl you really are. If you want to make constructive sense, hit the keys you know are right, and learn to hit them every time and rapidly.

" Faith without works is dead."—JAMES 2 : 20.

A PRAYER

"Deliver us from evil."

Jesus, our Friend and Saviour,—we thank Thee for Thy love. We thank Thee that Thy thoughts are with us; that young folks have a real place in Thy plan; that Thou art interested in our work and play, in our school and home, in our pets.

Please make all things right and give us wisdom to live according to Thy teaching for we know Thy way is best.

As we have faith in Thy love and teachings, give us strength and the desire to so work and play that any idea of wrong will be shunned. Help us to know the right and keep us faithful in doing it, today, that in the years to come we shall be just and honorable as we follow the counsel of Jesus. Amen.

A Message from Our Bible

"Hearken, my beloved brethren, hath not God chosen the poor of this world, rich in faith, and heirs of the kingdom which he hath promised to them that love him?

What doth it profit, my friends, though a man say he hath faith, and have not works? can faith save him?

A man may say, Thou hast faith, and I have works; show me thy faith without thy works, and I will show thee my faith by my works.

For as the body without the spirit is dead, so faith, without works is dead also."—From James 2.

9
FIGHTING SHADOWS

Did you ever get all gooseflesh, and feel your hair rise up on your head just because you suddenly caught a glimpse of your shadow at night? Sometimes when you walk across a street toward a store you see your reflection or shadow in the large plate glass window. I have seen birds throw themselves at a window, again and again; they would hit the window and fly away then come back, pecking and clawing. I am told that a grosbeak will do this for an hour or two,—just because he saw his shadow on that window glass and he thought it was another grosbeak. If he had seen a crow or a robin or a canary in the window the grosbeak would not have bothered about it!

Like shadows, most of the things we get upset about are not very real or important, certainly not worth fighting.

I have seen children get so upset and make all kinds of fuss because they were asked to do an errand. Of course they did the errand and usually they come back with a dime or some cookies or candy, and smiling happily.

Sometimes boys and girls get mad at someone and when they are asked what it is all about they really don't know. At least it's something very trivial and unreal, like your shadow. The best thing to do is to forget it before, like the grosbeak, they hurt themselves.

I think it might be a good idea to hang a picture of a cardinal grosbeak in your dining room so that you don't spend too much time fighting shadows.

"He that is slow to anger is better than the mighty."
—Proverbs 16:32.

A PRAYER

"THINE is the kingdom."

Our Father in heaven,—we greatly appreciate Thy loving care toward us. As Thy kingdom is an example for us, may we so live in our home and community, at work and at play, as to promote Thy will and Thy love among us.

Teach us to be kind and friendly, as Jesus always was, slow to anger and filled with the desire to show mercy.

We believe that Thou dost live within our hearts and as we care for, and so make strong, our bodies, we can the better serve Thee and become a real force for the building of Thy kingdom in our community and in the world through the teachings of Jesus our Lord. Amen.

A MESSAGE FROM OUR BIBLE

"Commit thy works unto the Lord, and thy thoughts shall be established.

He that handleth a matter wisely shall find good: and whoso trusteth in the Lord, happy is he.

Understanding is a wellspring of life unto him that hath it;

The heart of the wise teacheth his mouth, and addeth learning to his lips.

Pleasant words are as an honeycomb, sweet to the soul, and health;

He that is slow to anger is better than the mighty; and he that ruleth his spirit than he that taketh a city."—From PROVERBS 16.

COLORS

When God made this world of nature and animals and man He created many, many colors. One look at all the nations' flags reveals the great beauty of colors.

However, the girls know that there are many colors they cannot wear on their dress or in their hair. Some colors just can't seem to get along with each other. So when mother wants to redecorate the living room she is very careful to pick out the right colored wall paper to go well with the draperies and the chair upholstery.

Now go out into your garden in August where there are all kinds of flowers, and, of course, these flowers are of almost every color. Why is it that these flower colors do not clash? Perhaps we do not really know but we believe it is because the green in the stems and in the leaves and in the grass around them neutralizes the colors,—that is the green blends in with the colors so they do not clash.

Jesus has taught us that Christianity will do that for people. Whenever there is friction between friends it is a good plan to remember that " God so loved the world " that He sent Jesus to teach us how to get along happily with one another.

Sometimes we hear people say they don't like the negro! When people say *that*, it's because they don't have enough Christianity. All kinds and colors of people should live together peacefully and happily because of the effect that Christianity has upon their attitude.

" *God so loved the world . . .*"—John 3: 16.

A PRAYER

" Thine is the power."

Father in heaven,—we thank Thee for Thy friendliness toward us as shown in Jesus. To all people He spoke a kind word, and Thou didst always give Him the strength He needed to meet all troubles.

Through His example we ask that Thy power may give us the courage to express Christian love when others about us may be indifferent and neglectful.

Help us, dear God, to know how to be better young folks in our country by the same method Thou didst teach Thy son Jesus, who, in turn, has taught us to show friendliness to all people. Amen.

A Message from Our Bible

" As Moses lifted up the serpent in the wilderness, even so must the son of man be lifted up;

That whosoever believeth in him should not perish, but have eternal life.

For God so loved the world, that he gave his only begotten Son that whosoever believeth in him should not perish, but have everlasting life.

For God sent not his Son into the world to condemn the world; but that the world through him might be saved."—From John 3.

II

ANTITOXIN

Why does a person have that disease known as scarlet fever? The answer is quite simple. A scarlet fever germ gets into his system, and goes roaming all around until finally it has left hundreds of tiny germs all through his blood. But as soon as this bad germ gets a foothold in a boy's body his whole system begins to fight it off! His blood cells start at once to manufacture another germ to fight off and to try to kill the scarlet fever germ!

So the fight goes on, and just as when you work hard raking leaves or shoveling coal, you get all hot and tired, with that fight going on inside, you become very hot and tired—and when you are hot and tired inside you say you are sick.

If you should have scarlet fever the doctor would come and tell you to go to bed—even if you didn't want to—so that those good germs would have a chance to fight off the bad ones. The doctor even helps those good germs by feeding them some kind of medicine. These good germs and the medicine are called antitoxin because they fight against that poisonous or toxic germ, and when you get well after about five weeks you have so much antitoxin or friendly germs in your body that you will never have scarlet fever again!

When you think sometimes that you don't like a certain person and perhaps start talking about him or her, try letting the thought of Jesus, or your Sunday school class lesson, come into your mind and chase out all wrong ideas. Try not to let those bad thoughts get started and then you won't be troubled and bothered.

"*I am the way and the truth.*"—JOHN 14:6.

A PRAYER

"Thine is the glory."

Dear God,—we thank Thee for Jesus our Great Friend, who taught us to care for our health in order that we may be strong, and thus able to work for Thee.

We thank Thee for the help that doctors and nurses can give, and for parents and friends who watch over us.

This is a beautiful world, made so by the glory of Thy love in giving Jesus to us to show us the true way to live, as workers together, and for each other. Amen.

A Message from Our Bible

" Jesus said, I am the way, the truth, and the life; no man cometh unto the Father, but by me.

Verily I say unto you, He that believeth on me, the works that I do shall he do also; and greater works, because I go unto my Father.

And whatsoever ye shall ask in my name, that will I do, that the Father may be glorified in the Son.

If ye shall ask any thing in my name, I will do it.

If ye love me, keep my commandments."—From John 14.

TONE

At an entertainment some time ago I saw a row of very beautiful bells—about fifteen or twenty of them, and all different sizes. Pretty soon a man came in and began hitting those bells and each had a different tone so that very soon I realized he was playing a popular tune by striking certain bells. The small bells had a high tone and the larger ones were lower in tone.

It reminded me that once when I was a small boy I went on a picnic and as we finished our lunch and sat around the picnic table we began tapping the water glasses we had brought with us, and each seemed to have a different tone. This caused some interest so we tried to play a tune and someone discovered that he could get a lower tone by putting some sand in the glass that already had some water in it. The high tones came from the almost empty glasses or the ones which had very little clear water in them. So we tried to think we had all the tones of the scale. I couldn't help noticing that the more mud we had in the glass the lower was the tone.

Well, that's about the way with your town, or your school or any organization to which you may belong. The tone or standing is high or low according to the cleanness of the individual people who live there. I like to see a community and a home whose members observe Sunday as the Lord's Day. It raises the tone of a whole village or city.

"*Remember the sabbath day to keep it holy.*"—Exodus 20:8.

To Remember

"The Lord is my Shepherd."

A PRAYER

Dear God our Father,—we thank Thee for the leadership of Thy Son Jesus whose message leads us, as a shepherd directs his sheep, in safe paths. Make us want to follow the way He guides.

We thank Thee that life is not monotonous, but as the many tones give beautiful music, so there are many ways in which we can serve Thee in our home and community.

As Jesus taught us reverence toward Thee, help us to make our Lord's Day a holy day of remembrance, that through the week we shall have strength and purpose to follow Thy leadership.

A Message from Our Bible

" Remember the sabbath day to keep it holy.

Six days shalt thou labour, and do all thy work.

But the seventh day is the sabbath of the Lord thy God; in it thou shalt not do any work.

For in six days the Lord made heaven and earth, the sea and all that in them is and rested the seventh day: wherefore the Lord blessed the sabbath day, and hallowed it."—From Exodus 20.

" The sabbath was made for man, and not man for the sabbath.

Therefore the Son of man is Lord also of the sabbath."—From Mark 2.

MAGNETIC POWER

You all know what a magnet is—a piece of iron containing loadstone which has the power of attracting other iron to it.

If a person gets a piece of steel in his flesh, the doctor may use a magnet to draw it out. I know a man who, while working at his bench, got a tiny piece of steel in his eye. It was terribly painful and before it could be removed the doctor had to take him to Boston where a specialist made an incision behind the eye and then with the use of a great magnet the tiny speck was drawn out.

I think it's a lot of fun to play with a magnet. I have one of those magnet hammers and I like to use it to pick up tacks and small nails with, but I have noticed that it does not pick up a rusty nail.

That magnetic power will travel through a nail and attach another nail to it—but it won't travel through a rusty nail.

A knife blade has no magnetic power—but draw it a few times across that hammer and IT becomes a magnet!

So on Sundays, especially around Easter time, I think how in His great power of love Jesus drew those disciples to Him, and how people in turn since, and today, just naturally turn to Him and to those who know Him for help and advice, for Christ's power works through you and me if we are not rusty with wrong and evil and selfishness and indifference.

"—*I will draw all men to me.*"—JOHN 12:32.

To Remember

" The Lord is my shepherd; I shall not want."

A PRAYER

Dear Lord, our Good Shepherd,—we love Thee because Thou dost love us and care for us.

We thank Thee for Christian parents whom Thou hast taught to love us and comfort us when we are hurt, and care for us when we are sick. Help us to show our appreciation to them, and please bless them.

Dear God, help the people of other nations who are suffering, and the many who are starving. Show us how we may give them the things they need. Make us Thy helpers in comforting them with our friendship, and with our playthings and grant that we may teach them of Thy love that they may live in peace when they grow up, and turn to Thee for guidance, accepting Thee as their great Shepherd. Amen.

A Message from Our Bible

" If any man serve me, let him follow me; and where I am, there shall also my servant be; if any man serve me, him will my Father honour.

Father, glorify thy name. Then came a voice from heaven saying, I have both glorified it and will glorify it again.

Jesus said, This voice came not because of me, but for your sakes.

I, if I be lifted up from the earth, will draw all men unto me."—From John 12.

ENVELOPES

When you send a sealed envelope to your friend seventy miles away, you are quite sure no one will open it and read its contents except that person to whom it is addressed.

So when you pray to God about some tough problem that bothers you, you close your eyes and your message goes directly to Him—and if you have faith you will know that He sends His advice right back to you. Prayer is just between you and God.

Envelopes are useful for a lot of things; and they are not always made of paper. A doctor puts pills in them and leaves them on the table with directions, when you are sick—or if it is liquid medicine he puts it in a glass envelope which you call a bottle.

Your mother may can vegetables and fruits in jars and tins; these are envelopes too.

When visiting a laboratory once I saw a lot of bottles with wiggly, tiny living creatures in them. I was strictly warned not to touch those bottle envelopes for they contained germs and the doctors were watching their development—and to open the envelopes might mean the spread of some terrible disease.

That made me think of gossip—throwing stories we may have heard,—around other people, which might not be true, and which might destroy good friendship. So when you feel the urge to say something bad about others just stop and seal it up as in an envelope—or perhaps send the message to God so that no one else can read it.

"*Let him refrain his lips that he speaks no guile.*"— I Peter 3:10.

To Remember

"He maketh me to lie down in green pastures."

A PRAYER

DEAR Friend Jesus,—we thank Thee so much, for the friendliness Thou hast shown, giving an example for us to live by. We thank Thee for the interest Thou hast shown toward young folks, regardless of race or color.

Teach us to have Thy spirit of consideration, that we may play together without thought of discord.

In times of weakness make us strong with thoughts of Thee, so that no matter what others may say, we may not lose our temper lest we speak too hastily.

We look to Thee in prayer and worship for guidance to right man and womanhood. Amen.

A Message from Our Bible

"Be ye all of one mind, having compassion one of another; love as brothers, be pitiful, be courteous;

For he that will love life and see good days, let him refrain his tongue from evil; and his lips that they speak no guile;

Let him shun evil and do good; let him speak peace and follow it.

For the eyes of the Lord are over the righteous and his ears are open unto their prayers; but the face of the Lord is against them that do evil;

Sanctify the Lord God in your hearts."—From I PETER 3.

ELECTRIC LIGHT BULBS

Let us imagine a boy who had never seen electric lights, and when he saw, in your garage, a glass globe hanging from the ceiling he asked what in the world that was hanging there for! So you turned the light switch and he was amazed. I think our visitor would ask you what was inside that globe. So you told him "wires," and when he went home he got a glass jar and threw in some wires—but no light came! Or he might pick up the electric heater and carry it out and set it in the dog house and wonder why it didn't heat that little room!

That globe lights when those tiny wires are so placed inside that they are in direct touch with a power that energizes them—and even if we go to the powerhouse and look at the turbines we don't see any power! But when those tiny wires light up you know there is power—that bulb shows it.

When I see boys and girls stop their play and run to the store or to a neighbor's on an errand for their mother, without complaining I know they have the power of God, giving them the desire to be helpful, to be unselfish, which is the light of Christianity shining through them.

Jesus was that kind of a boy and God depended on Him and depends on you to carry His message of love and usefulness to enlighten the world.

"*Ye are the light of the world.*"—Matthew 5 : 14.

To Remember

"He leadeth me beside the still waters."

A PRAYER

Lead us, O Lord, by Thy hand and in so doing electrify our lives with Thy light and power, that we, like Thee, may have the ability to serve Thee by showing others the path of Thy love.

Lead us, O Christ, every day, all day, quietly in the way of truth and honor and service. Give us a willing mind to run errands for those who are busy or old, for in so doing we please Thee.

Let the principle of Thy love, O God, fill us with determination to live the Christian way that peace on this earth may be established, and Thy will be done. Amen.

A Message from Our Bible

"Ye are the light of the world. A city that is set on a hill cannot be hid.

Neither do men light a candle, and put it under a bushel, but on a candlestick; and it giveth light unto all that are in the house.

Let your light so shine before men, that they may see your good works, and glorify your Father which is in heaven."—From Matthew 5.

LEAVES OF A BOOK

WHILE sitting at mother's desk, one day, a boy spilled some black ink on page 197 of a very interesting and worth-while book. He quickly used the blotting paper and he was happy to see that the words under the blot of ink could still be read! Then he thought how terribly that spot looked, so finally he just took hold of that page and tore it out. Of course by tearing out that whole leaf it took two pages of the story away and when the next person read the book and came to this place he found that on those missing pages was the author's solution to the many questions he had discussed in the previous 196 pages! In fact, to tear out any page would destroy much of the value of a book.

Probably one or two of you,—not many!—read the "funnies" in the daily papers. You can hardly wait to see how Oaky or Jane or Superman is going to get out of that terrible trouble. Today's paper is to tell the solution and save the situation. So you rush in from school at noon and ask where the paper is only to find that someone used it to kindle the fire in the fireplace!

Well, isn't a Sunday school class something like a book —if one person misses, it just spoils the chance of having a "banner class." It's the same with the church service, —if someone stays at home God must feel hurt for His church is just so much less effective.

Let us consider this country of ours a great book also, —there are black leaves, there are red leaves, brown leaves as well as white,—people of all races and creeds; each are important and should not be blotted or torn.

"Destroy not the work of God."—ROMANS 14:20.

[31]

To Remember

" He restoreth my soul."

A PERSONAL PRAYER

Dear Father, if I have done or said things today that have hurt someone, please forgive me, and help me make it right before I sleep tonight. I'm so thoughtless sometimes! Help me to have the considerate character of Jesus who always went about doing good and speaking praise.

Give me strength for tomorrow, dear Lord, that no minute will be blotted with unkindness, no hour with idleness.

Teach me to be strong to resist, when others may try to influence me to wrong deeds, or turn me away from the path of right.

Bless this home, dear God, and those who love me; and give me many opportunities to show my appreciation. Amen.

A Message from Our Bible

"We shall all stand before the judgment seat of Christ.

So then every one of us shall give account of himself to God.

Let us not therefore judge one another any more; but judge this rather, that no man put a stumblingblock or an occasion to fall in his brother's way.

For the kingdom of God is not meat and drink; but righteousness, and peace, and joy in the Holy Spirit.

For he that in these things serveth Christ is acceptable to God, and approved of men.

Destroy not the work of God."—From Romans 14.

PENDULUM

I THINK I had better talk to you about pendulums now, because in a few years more children will be asking: " Mr. Sargent, what is a pendulum? " Like people, there are apparently no two pendulums alike; and like people some are slow; some are fast. No one thinks much about the pendulum of a clock, they all do the same thing over and over: they just go from here to there, from here to there, monotonously!

Imagine yourself just going from home to school; from school to home—and never breaking over to go to a circus, or a party, or a movie or skating! I think if a pendulum could talk it would say: " Let me swing way over just once—or even give an extra distance to my swing." But no, all it does is just to go from here to there, from here to there!

If that pendulum SHOULD go " haywire " or stop,—everything would stop—or be wrong. You'd be late for school; Dad might be late to the office.—The only time we seem to think about pendulums is when the hands of the clock stop moving,—or they go too fast or too slow!

A lot of people would not make good pendulums because they like to be admired, or praised, and coaxed—they are just too selfish; but we all respect those people who work steadily and unselfishly for God and His church, loyally doing their work in keeping Christianity alive so that their village or city may be clean and on a high level—pendulum sort of people, dependable even without being " show-offs," or scarcely recognized.

"*He that doeth the will of God, abideth.*"—I JOHN 2 : 17.

To Remember

"He leadeth me in the paths of righteousness for his name's sake."

A PRAYER

DEAR Lord, we thank Thee for our church and for its leaders who work hard that its influence may be felt far and wide. Give us the sense of true and faithful loyalty, that we may never shirk our responsibilities.

There are many things we can do, and thus show our desire to help spread Thy gospel to all nations.

Lead us, O God, in Thy way of love and even though we are young we can help make Thy kingdom seen as a pattern for this world.

Teach us, dear Lord, to be more like Thee, for Thy name's sake. Amen.

A Message from Our Bible

" He that saith, I know him, and keepeth not his commandments, the truth is not in him.

But whoso keepeth his word, in him verily is the love of God perfected: hereby know we that we are in him.

He that saith he abideth in him ought himself also so to walk,—

He that loveth his brother abideth in the light, and there is none occasion of stumbling in him.

He that doeth the will of God abideth for ever."— From I JOHN 2.

THREE SHINGLES

Big drops of water were fast pouring through the roof of my garage during a recent rainstorm, so I went hunting for a leak in the roof. I soon discovered a place where I could see light through the shingles and so I went out onto the roof and easily found the leak where there were only two shingles.

You see it takes three shingles to keep a roof from leaking—two shingles must be laid first, side by side, as closely together as possible, and then one more shingle must be placed over these two in such a position as to cover the little crack where the first two come together.— I remember we used to call this "breaking joints"—ask your father to explain that to you.

Now each one of those three shingles is just as important as the other, but all three are necessary and must work together if the roof is to shed rain and not leak.

It's really three snowflakes that keep the ground warm in winter—if the flakes just piled up one on top of the other they would make stacks and the cold air would rush down between these stacks, but the flakes overlap and make a tight blanket because they "break joint."

God depends upon your loyalty to Him, but He also needs your co-operation with other people—that is why we have the church. Christian boys and girls and men and women working together for God can cover the world with the warmth and protection of Christianity.

"*Go ye therefore and teach all nations.*"—Matthew 28:19.

[35]

To Remember

"Yea, though I walk through the valley of the shadow of death I will fear no evil."

A PRAYER

Our Father in heaven, we thank Thee for Thy message of love,—because of it this has been a happy home. In our work and in our play we have tried to honor Thee.

Dear Lord, make all homes happy.

In times of sorrow and anxiety because of dangers that some are facing, please comfort them and give them courage, that they may have hope.

Help all who are sick or lonely, and use us to carry joy and sunshine, in order to cheer them.

Make us worthy and use us in Thy plan in making this world a Christian place that all may know true happiness. Amen.

A Message from Our Bible

"And Jesus spake unto them, saying, All power is given unto me in heaven and in earth.

Go ye therefore, and teach all nations, baptizing them in the name of the Father, and of the Son, and of the Holy Spirit;

Teaching them to observe all things whatsoever I have commanded you; and, lo, I am with you alway, even unto the end of the world."—From Matthew 28.

19
DOLLAR SIGNS

SOME time ago I read in the daily paper an incident about a very poor family. The father and mother wanted to give their children Christmas presents and have a nice dinner that day of days. So they sold the one good piece of furniture in their house—a desk that was given to the mother long ago, for ten dollars! Thinking they would get three nice new crisp one-dollar bills for the children, they took the ten-dollar bill to the bank. It was counterfeit.

I am told there are men in Washington who can tell a counterfeit bill with their eyes closed! The texture and treatment of a real bill is such that they can tell at once it is genuine.

People, sometimes, are like dollar signs—$—some are selfish and so they talk big and try to make people think they are more important than they really are. Sometimes they look down on other people and think they are a little better than the colored boy or the poor girl.

God can always tell by the texture of your thoughtfulness and your treatment of others just how genuine you are—and so, often, can your parents and your minister.

If you want to keep in circulation and be popular and have many friends—be yourself, wholesome, trustworthy, honest and unselfish toward those whom you can help.

"If a person thinks himself something when he isn't— he just fools himself."—GALATIANS 6:3 (paraphrased).

To Remember

"For thou art with me."

A PRAYER

We thank Thee, dear God, that Jesus was a child like us, and that He understands our foolish ways.

As He was strong enough to overcome temptations, so are we if we will keep Him in mind, close beside us in our heart at all times.

Make us genuine, dear Lord; sincere and trustworthy, and lead us to be generous and unselfish as Jesus always was.

In our play help us to be careful in the words we use, and keep us from being bold, and thoughtless or hateful. Keep our minds from evil, and lead us in the right we pray in Jesus' name. Amen.

A Message from Our Bible

" Bear ye one another's burdens, and so fulfil the law of Christ.

For if a man think himself to be something, when he is nothing he deceiveth himself.

Let every man prove his own work, and then shall he have rejoicing in himself alone, and not in another.

For every man shall bear his own burden.

For whatsoever a man soweth, that shall he also reap.

As we have therefore opportunity, let us do good unto all."—From GALATIANS 6.

NAILS INSIDE TREES

"Look out for the fishbones, now." Have you boys and girls ever heard those words before? After you've been fishing all day and you have brought home two or three nice trout—and there they are right before you brown and hot, and you are just about starved,—then mother or dad reminds you to look out for the bones! To be sure, it takes away a lot of joy but it may save much pain later.

Somehow we often hear of fishbones, and marbles and even pins getting inside of small boys and girls—and I expect it's because they swallowed them! But who ever heard of a tree swallowing a nail?

Nevertheless, when my father and I were once sawing a big log in two with one of those go-to-you-come-to-me saws we suddenly heard a terrible "squawk"—and sure enough it had struck a nail right in the middle of that log. Yes, sir! It seemed as though that tree must have swallowed that nail.

I remember my dad telling me how that nail got there. He said that without a doubt someone, many, many years before, had driven a nail into that tree and had forgotten to pull it out—and now, years later, it spoiled a nice sharp saw.

I saw a boy get hit by a branch of a tree right across his ear. He was all right for several years and then he began to be deaf in that ear, and soon lost the hearing entirely.

If you really mean business and want to help make a better world, one that is peace-loving and clean—ask your parents to help you keep from driving nails into your character now while you are young—nails such as selfish ideas, wrong habits, and bad language, etc.—and remember always to pray, so that you can say as David once said:

"*O God, thou hast taught me from my youth.*"— PSALM 71:17.

To Remember

" Thy rod and thy staff they comfort me."

A PERSONAL PRAYER

I come to Thee now, dear Lord, at the close of a happy day, to thank Thee for the joy that has been mine in all my work and play.

I thank Thee for my home and those who watch over me. Make me worthy of their love, and Thine.

Now as I sleep, dear God, I leave everything in Thy care, trusting Thee to keep safe those whom I love, and give us all peaceful rest.

In the beauty of a new day, give me strength and cheerfulness, that I may give joy tomorrow, to any who may be sad, or heedless, or sick, that this community may be a little better because I'm a part of it, and so guide me, and bless us all. Amen.

A Message from Our Bible

" In thee, O Lord, do I put my trust;
For thou art my hope, O Lord God;
My mouth shall shew forth thy righteousness and thy salvation all the day; for I know not the numbers thereof.

I will go in the strength of the Lord God; I will make mention of thy righteousness, even of thine only.

O God, thou hast taught me from my youth; and hitherto have I declared thy wondrous works."—From Psalm 71.

SMUDGES

A YOUNG lad came home from school almost in tears. He handed his mother a white sheet of paper with some writing on it and in one corner in red pencil " 85 "! " We had an examination today," said the boy, " and all my answers are correct. Why did I get ' 85 ' and not ' 100 ' ? "

Mother looked the paper all through and came to a smudge on that nice white sheet. " There is your trouble," she said. " Miss J. took 15 off for lack of neatness! "

You see, one word had been spelled wrongly, or poorly written, so the boy tried to erase it—and left a smudge.

I'm sure it would have been better to have drawn one or two lines through the mistake and then have written beside it or above it, the right word. I think, if he had done that, his " score " would have been " 100."

People expect to see a mistake now and then; if it is properly corrected they don't mind so much, but I guess we all hate smudges!

God hates smudges too. It's a sin to lie, and cheat, and to disobey, and sometimes a boy or girl does so and then, when found out, lies to get out of it; or tries to lay it onto someone else. In God's sight that's a smudge. So, it seems to me, the thing to do, if you do wrong, is just admit it, draw a line through it by saying you are terribly sorry, and make amends by doing the right thing.

God disapproves of a smudger,—but if you admit you are wrong and by repentance cross it off and do right, He will give you a clean sheet and a high marking score.

"*I have sinned against heaven and against thee.*"— LUKE 15:18.

To Remember

"Thou preparest a table before me in the presence of mine enemies."

A PERSONAL PRAYER

I thank Thee, dear God, for being so patient with me. So often I have done wrong and said mean things that have hurt the feelings of others. Give me courage to make everything right with them, that all may be happy again.

Thy great love is able to forgive, please give me enough to so act as to be worthy of forgiveness.

Even in the midst of His enemies, Jesus refused to retaliate, or lose control. I pray that I may be like Him, and so be helpful in making peace and happiness real among all the nations on earth.

Bless this home, dear Lord, and all my friends, and be near to all people everywhere, in Thy name and for our sakes I pray. Amen.

A Message from Our Bible

"I will arise and go to my father, and will say unto him, Father, I have sinned against heaven, and before thee.

And am no more worthy to be called thy son; make me as one of thy hired servants.

And he arose, and came to his father. But when he was yet a great way off, his father saw him, and had compassion, and ran, and fell on his neck, and kissed him.

This my son was dead, and is alive again; he was lost, and is found. And they began to be merry."—From the story of the prodigal son, LUKE 15.

22
A WEATHER VANE

When you want to find a weather vane to know in which direction the wind is blowing,—you look to the top of a garage, a barn or perhaps a church steeple, and there you will often see a rooster, as atop the steeple of Sailor's Rest in Boston, or a horse, a fish or possibly just an arrow. You can easily tell the direction of the wind because the rooster or fish or arrow is heading into it. That is,—if the wind is blowing from the east the weather vane points toward the east—and people will say, "The wind's in the east, I guess it's going to rain." Or when it points north it's a north wind so it will doubtless be pleasant weather for a few hours.

A weather vane heads into the wind—toward the source of power. Abraham Lincoln was that kind of man; whenever he saw a hard task, or a disagreeable one, he headed right into it—and saw it through, and got it done.

Jesus was that kind of person. When He saw temptation He set His face against it, and fought it back so it wouldn't get a start as a habit in His life. And when He saw other people in trouble and afraid He went to them and helped them stand erect and gave them courage to face whatever task they had to do.

Sometimes people take the easy way and just limply go WITH the wind—doing what everyone else does even if it's wrong. Sort of wishy-washy folks! When a weather vane does that we know something is wrong with it—it needs oiling, or it's bent and twisted.

It's often hard to be a Christian when the current of habits goes the other way,—but the pride and welfare of our country depends upon young folks facing hard tasks—heading and walking toward God, the source of all power.

"*Looking unto Jesus the author and finisher of our faith.*"—Hebrews 12:2.

To Remember

" Thou anointest my head with oil."

A PRAYER

HELP us, dear Lord, to better understand Thy great love. As Thou didst live for others, teach us also to be unselfish. Give us the willingness to share our playthings with boys and girls who are less fortunate, and to sacrifice for those who are in need of what we might be able to give.

Give us courage to set the right example even when others try to turn us away from the true course we had planned, in the name of Jesus. Amen.

A Message from Our Bible

" Let us run with patience the race that is set before us,

Looking unto Jesus the author, and finisher of our faith; who for the joy that was set before him endured the cross,—and is set down at the right hand of the throne of God.

Despise not thou the chastening of the Lord, nor faint when thou art rebuked of him;

For whom the Lord loveth he chasteneth,

If ye endure chastening God dealeth with you as with sons; for what son is he whom the father chasteneth not?

Make straight paths for your feet, lest that which is lame is turned out of the way;

Follow peace with all men, and holiness, without which no man shall see the Lord."—From HEBREWS 12.

HINGES

We went over to our farm in Bath, New Hampshire, recently and while roaming about the house we saw a big box in the storeroom. In moving it, Bob and I discovered it was quite heavy, so we tried to lift up the hinged cover to see what it might contain. What a squeaking, squawking noise came from those hinges as we, with difficulty, raised that cover two or three inches.

Of course we could have opened that cover wide up, but it would have damaged the box, or broken the hinges. So I got some oil and poured it on them, and carefully scraped away some of the rust, until at last those hinges worked almost as good as new.

Occasionally a door in your house will squeak, and when it is opened it seems to say, "O I hate to work; why don't you leave me alone?" "Get into the room some other way,—don't bother me." Then someone quickly gets the oil can.

Often, when at the farm, I'll wake up in the middle of the night and hear a terrible noise,—I'm sure it's a ghost and know the place must be haunted. How interesting! But shucks! it's only a window shutter swinging back and forth in the wind on squeaking, rusty hinges!

Why do hinges squeak? I think there are two reasons: one is because of lack of use and so they become rusty, and the other is that they lack oil.

God depends upon you and me to keep active in building a better world. Jesus is our example. He went to church, and was always doing good so that no rust of evil and wrong and selfish habits ever slowed Him down or caused Him to shirk,—indeed He kept Himself fit and strong and ready with the oil of prayer and reverence.

"*I have confidence in you, through the Lord.*"—Galatians 5:10.

[45]

To Remember
" My cup runneth over."

A PRAYER

Dear God, teach us to appreciate all Thou hast given the people of this world—the beauty of flowers, the joy of snow, the love of parents, the happiness of friendships. Help us so to live the Christian way, that others may feel a confidence in us at all times.

Let not little quarrels and harsh words mar our friendships, or cause sadness in our home.

Help us to always keep close to Thee in prayer and through our church worship, and make us ever willing and eager to be of service whenever we are asked, in Jesus' name. Amen.

A Message from Our Bible

" Stand fast therefore in the liberty wherewith Christ hath made us free, and be not entangled again with the yoke of bondage.

For, ye have been called unto liberty; only use not liberty for an occasion to the flesh, but by love serve one another.

For all the law is fulfilled in one word, even in this; thou shalt love thy neighbour as thyself.

I have confidence in you through the Lord, that ye will be none otherwise minded;

For we through the Spirit wait for the hope of righteousness by faith."—From Galatians 5.

DOORKNOBS

Close your eyes. Now, how many doors are there in the room in which you are sitting? Probably, each one of those doors has a doorknob so that you can open the door as you leave the room and when someone wants to come in he can turn the knob from the outside and open the door.

Even outside doors have doorknobs or some handle device to lift the latch. Doorknobs are on both sides of doors so that one can go in and out whenever he wants to.

But there is a very beautiful painting which, I am sure, most of you have seen. It's the painting of a door, and Jesus, holding high a lantern, is knocking. One thing is missing on that door. There is a grating so that people inside may look out and see who is knocking, but there is no handle or doorknob!

That door at which Jesus is knocking can only be opened from the inside. Indeed the artist, Mr. William Holman Hunt, desired to show by this painting how Christ stands at the door of your life waiting for you to let Him in.

I am told that when the artist had finished this painting a friend said to him, "You haven't finished your work, Mr. Hunt; there is no handle on the door."

"That," said Mr. Hunt, "is the door to the human heart; it can only be opened from within."

In like manner when you go to God in prayer He will open the door and hear you, for Jesus once told us to

---

"*Knock, and it shall be opened unto you.*"—Luke 11:9.

To Remember

"Surely goodness and mercy shall follow me all the days of my life."

A PRAYER

Dear God, our Father, as we face a new day, give us courage and willingness to do any disagreeable task that knocks at our door and which needs to be done.

Through Thy great goodness and mercy we know Thou wilt help us in our studies and guide us in our play each day.

Grant Thy blessing to those who do not know Thee so well and lead us to teach them about prayer, and the love of Jesus for all, and bless the homes of all Thy children and keep the nations at peace with each other forever. Amen.

A Message from Our Bible

" Ask and it shall be given you; seek and ye shall find; knock and it shall be opened unto you.

For every one that asketh receiveth; and he that seeketh findeth; and to him that knocketh it shall be opened.

If a son shall ask bread of any of you that is a father, will he give him a stone? Or if he ask a fish, will he for a fish give him a serpent?

Or if he shall ask an egg, will he offer him a scorpion?

If ye then, being evil, know how to give good gifts unto your children how much more shall your heavenly Father give the Holy Spirit to them that ask him? "—Luke 11.

25

STEEPLES

At each Christmas time I remember when I was a very small boy how glad I used to be that our house had a chimney, not because it carried the smoke away, but so that Santa Claus could get in on Christmas eve!

Does your church have a tall steeple? Why?

We often think of steeples on a church as signifying that everything about that church points to God,—just as the steeple seems to lift its finger heavenward. But God isn't staying up there all the time, in fact I like to think of Him as being down here near us, right where we are, walking by our side and sitting beside us if we let Him.

So when I see a steeple I don't think of it as pointing to God, but rather as an aerial reaching out to catch the message of God and of Jesus, and bringing it down through our church that all may hear it and desire to invite God to walk by our side always and so enthuse us to go out and tell others about Jesus.

If we didn't have the church we wouldn't have a Christian country. Therefore the steeple seems to say: " Come and hear what God wants of you, for His message is coming in."

Let us also be as steeples, aerials for God to catch His message and then live it with others to make a better world.

"Enter into his gates with thanksgiving, and into his courts with praise."—Psalm 100:4.

To Remember

"—and I will dwell in the house of the Lord forever."

A PERSONAL PRAYER

Use me, dear Lord, as Thy messenger, to carry Thy gospel of love to so many who seem not to know it.

Keep me patient and free from quarrels, that I may lead others into Thy church where we all may hear Thy word and praise Thy name.

Lead me, O Christ, to dedicate my whole life to Thy service through my play, my studies and the work that I shall choose.

Please bless this home and those who watch over me, and who love me as I love them, in Christ's name I ask Thee this. Amen.

A Message from Our Bible

" Make a joyful noise unto the Lord, all ye lands.

Serve the Lord with gladness; come before his presence with singing. Know ye that the Lord he is God; it is he that hath made us, and not we ourselves; we are his people, and the sheep of his pasture.

Enter into his gates with thanksgiving, and into his courts with praise; be thankful unto him, and bless his name.

For the Lord is good; his mercy is everlasting; and his truth endureth to all generations."—Psalm 100.

MODELS

ON the cover of magazines, sometimes, there is the picture of a boy. When I see that boy with a fish pole, and worms wriggling out of a box in his pocket, and above all with a dirty face and perhaps a finger with a soiled piece of cloth around it, and leading a bicycle with a flat tire—and, O yes, a flea-scratching dog,—I wonder who was the model or pattern the artist looked at when he drew it!

I have often stood looking at the Statue of Liberty. It is an inspiration just to think about it, for it stands for protection, for love, for security, and light to strangers, as well as Americans. I thought to myself, " Who but a mother could have been the model for that statue? " So I looked up the history of it and sure enough I discovered that the artist had for his model, his mother, Charlotte Beysser Bartholdi.

When I look at a boy or a girl I often wonder whose example makes him act or talk that way. What hero of that child developed such a clean, fine boy or girl? For the impression you make on other people reveals the influence of your home and your friends.

If we seriously want this world to really be a safe and happy place, you boys and girls will help make it so if you take Jesus as your model, and try your best to live like Him who was a living symbol of honor and Christian love.

" *And Jesus said, Follow me and I will make you fishers of men.*"—MATTHEW 4: 19.

To Remember

"Blessed are the poor in spirit for theirs is the kingdom of heaven."

A PERSONAL PRAYER

I THANK Thee, dear God, that so much joy comes to me each day. My puppy is so much fun, please don't ever let her be sick.

Even though I don't particularly like to go to school every day, my teachers are very nice, and they make my lessons interesting.

Help me to appreciate my happiness, and to show it to them who give it. Bless the children of other lands who have so few advantages and whose parents do not know about Thy love and watchful care.

Guide them to some mission church where they may learn of Thee through the message Thou hast taught in Jesus Christ. Amen.

A Message from Our Bible

" From that time Jesus began to preach, and to say,— Repent; for the kingdom of heaven is at hand.

The people which sat in darkness saw great light;

And Jesus, walking by the sea of Galilee saw two brethren, Simon called Peter, and Andrew his brother, casting a net into the sea; for they were fishers.

And he saith unto them, Follow me, and I will make you fishers of men.

And they left their nets and followed him.

And Jesus went about all Galilee, teaching, and preaching the gospel of the kingdom, and healing all manner of sickness."—From MATTHEW 4.

PICTURES

Have you a camera? Why do you take pictures? Why do you have a picture of your father and mother in your room? or of your brother in the armed services? or your friends?

I think it is because you love them and respect them.

Sometimes pictures help us. When a boy is thinking of doing something he knows is wrong,—one look at his mother's picture on his dresser may decide his actions in favor of the right.

A picture of a man in baseball uniform makes you want to go right out and pitch a no-hit, no-run game!

A librarian told me an incident of a boy who rushed into the library right after school each day—and ran to a certain book and turned the pages until he came to a certain place, then smiled with satisfaction and went out! One day the librarian followed him to the book and she heard him say: "Ah he hasn't caught him yet." She looked over his shoulder and saw a picture of a bull chasing a dog!

In the papers and magazines we see a lot of pictures.— They are meant to influence us, perhaps to fight, or sacrifice a bit harder, or to gain our sympathy.

I hope every boy's and every girl's room has in it a picture of Christ, and it would be nice to see a picture of your church there, as well as your father and mother, and other members of your family, and friends; and in that way show your young visitors the people and things you are proud of.

"*I have set the Lord ever before me.*"—Psalm 16: 8.

To Remember

"Blessed are they that mourn: for they shall be comforted."

A PRAYER

Dear God, we ask Thy healing blessing to be with all who are sick, especially with all who are crippled; and there are many people who are sad today; please look after them and give them happiness again.

Use us, dear Lord, and make us willing young folks, and cheerful as we help them who are in need. Thou hast set the example for us when all through Thy life Thou didst help all who were in any trouble. Teach us to radiate joy that others may find cheer. Amen.

A Message from Our Bible

" Preserve me, O God; for in thee do I put my trust.
I will bless the Lord who hath given me counsel;
I have set the Lord always before me: because he is at my right hand, I shall not be moved.
Therefore my heart is glad and my glory rejoiceth;
Thou wilt show me the path of life; in thy presence is fulness of joy; at thy right hand there are pleasures for evermore."—From Psalm 16.

BRIDGES

When you are walking along a road and come to a river how do you get over onto the other side? That's right of course,—over a bridge.

Now there are many kinds of bridges. There are great big steel and concrete ones. There are suspension bridges, covered wooden ones, and even rope bridges. There are pontoon bridges and sometimes when you go fishing you cross the stream on a log bridge! Then again, if the stream is narrow you just jump over and that makes it a "jump" or "air" bridge. But I've been particularly interested in the story of a silk bridge.

One time a spider sat on top of a little stick stuck upright in the ground near a stream. The water came up around it during the night and the spider was trapped. Although he was near the shore it was too far for him to jump. He couldn't quite reach a blade of grass that swayed quite close to him. So Mr. Spider just sat down to think!

Some people just sit and spin yarns, but our friend the spider spun a silken thread. He let that thread down and allowed it to sway in the breeze until it caught on the grass blade, and then the spider walked ashore!

All that God asks of us is that we do the best we can with what we have and He will help us over tough places and land us safely as wholesome, honest, clean young people.

Let us work faithfully *"to be accepted of God."*—II Corinthians 5:9.

To Remember

"Blessed are they which do hunger and thirst after righteousness: for they shall be filled."

A PRAYER

Dear God, we know Thy love for us is great, and may we learn how to appreciate it by showing our eagerness to apply it towards others.

At school and at home there are many ways to express that love. When things go wrong and we don't have our way, help us to stop and think before we speak.

What Thou dost think of us is more important than our personal desires, so give us the desire, we pray, to always think of Thee first in all our doings. Let us truly work faithfully that Thou wilt accept us as Thy messengers of love to all around us. Amen.

A Message from Our Bible

"Wherefore we labour, that we may be accepted of him.

For we must all appear before the judgment seat of Christ; that every one may receive the things done in his body, according to that he hath done, whether it is good or bad.

All things are of God who hath reconciled us to himself by Jesus Christ ——

Now then we are ambassadors for Christ ——

For we preach not ourselves, but Christ Jesus the Lord; and ourselves your servants for Jesus' sake.

For God, who commanded the light to shine out of darkness, hath shined in our hearts, to give the light of the knowledge of the glory of God in the face of Jesus Christ."—From II Corinthians 5.

FULL MEASURE

Why is it, when you go to the store to buy a half peck of potatoes, and the clerk puts them in a bag on the weighing machine, you like to watch that indicator? It isn't because you are afraid of being cheated! When it almost balances, but not quite, you wonder what he is going to do, and always the clerk puts in another potato bringing that indicator over the full measure mark. Or you go and ask for a pound of nails and the store man will throw in two or three nails to make sure it is full measure.

What is this full measure?

Each country has a standard measure,—the American yard is less than the French metre. The American dollar is less than the English pound,—and if I should offer an Englishman our standard dollar for his standard pound it would not be fair. Some day the world will have a single standard, and then it will be much easier to do business with each other and perhaps it will make the nations more friendly.

Now, God has a standard of measurement and it's meant for Russia as well as for America. It's just as wrong to lie and cheat in Mexico as it is in St. Johnsbury, or Bath, or Boston, or Washington, or Colorado Springs.

Men's laws may vary today but God's law of love and honor and right is for everyone in the world, and God sent His Son Jesus to us in order that He might teach us the living standard by which we are all measured.

"He makes his sun to rise on the good and evil; and sends rain on the just and the unjust."—Matthew 5:45.

To Remember

"Blessed are the meek, for they shall inherit the earth."

A PERSONAL PRAYER

Father in heaven, this is a beautiful world; and as I look at the stars at night, and the sun by day, and the trees that grow and the green grass or snow, I feel so humble in thinking of Thy greatness and Thy goodness.

Everything Thou hast made and caused to grow is for all who will recognize the beauty and usefulness of these things.

Teach me to play fair with Thee and to make use of Thy gifts, that all may find joy in these evidences of Thy great power meant for everyone. Keep me from selfishness I pray, in Jesus' name. Amen.

A Message from Our Bible

" Ye have heard that it hath been said, Thou shalt love thy neighbour and hate thine enemy.

But I say unto you, Love your enemies, bless them that curse you, do good to them that hate you, and pray for them which despitefully use you, and persecute you.

That ye may be the children of your Father which is in heaven; for he maketh his sun to rise on the evil and on the good, and sendeth rain on the just and on the unjust.

For if you love them which love you—

What do ye more than others?

Be ye therefore perfect, even as your Father which is in heaven is perfect."—From Matthew 5.

CABBAGES

Of all the vegetables that grow in the garden I think the cabbage is the most interesting. It looks something like a basketball, only it is green. First there is an outer coat of big leaves—like the shingles on a house they overlap each other as though they wanted to protect the inside from the storm and winds.

If we remove those outside leaves and look more deeply we see smaller ones laid carefully, overlapping each other and seeming to protect what is underneath. And so on it goes, each layer of leaves folded more tightly over the tender ones underneath.

Now these outside leaves seem to be a coat of armor to protect the inner ones from worms and bugs and hail. If the worms should reach the inside tender leaves we know, of course, that the whole cabbage is spoiled. Good, whole, unspotted outside leaves therefore tell us right away that the essential inner leaves are white and good.

That's exactly the way I can tell the kind of inner character a boy or girl has,—by the way he acts, by his language, by his disposition. If a boy is clean-spoken, if a girl is sweet-tempered at home and at play I know that the inner character of that boy or girl is clean and honest.

Keep yourselves " unspotted from the world."—James 1 : 27.

To Remember

" Blessed are the merciful; for they shall obtain mercy."

A PRAYER

Dear God, we thank Thee for the understanding we may have of the life of Jesus. He so clearly tells us how to live, by His own words and deeds.

Help us to apply His way to our everyday living in school, at home and on the playgrounds.

Teach us to be considerate of our companions, and, like Jesus, to think of all with whom we talk and play as our friends. Thus can we, as young folks, serve Thee in Christ's name. Amen.

A Message from Our Bible

" Every good gift and every perfect gift is from above, and cometh down from the Father.

Wherefore, my beloved, let every man be swift to hear, slow to speak, slow to wrath;

But be ye doers of the word, and not hearers only, deceiving your own selves.

If any man among you seem to be religious and bridleth not his tongue, but deceiveth his own heart, this man's religion is vain.

Pure religion and undefiled before God and the Father is this, To visit the fatherless and widows in their affliction, and to keep himself unspotted from the world."—From James i.

31
A PAIL OF WATER

"Pour some sweet cream in with it and perhaps it will take the sour taste away." That remark was made to a soda fountain clerk who discovered that a small amount of cream left in a bottle was sour.

I know where there is a well with beautifully clear, sweet water in it. But once when we tasted that water it was bitter; so we decided to wait a few weeks hoping that any foreign matter would disappear with the coming in of fresh water. But in a few weeks it was almost as bad though the well had filled to running over. So in the fall when the well was only one quarter full we dipped it all out and cleaned it.

When out fishing did you ever take off your shoes and play in a pool in the stream? and wonder why the water was so dirty when fresh water was running in all the time? Well, you see all that mud and dirt settled to the bottom and when you stepped in it stirred it all up. To make the pool clean you would have to hoe out all that mud.

You can't pour a pail of nice fresh clean water into a tub half filled with muddy, soapy water and make it good to drink! A pail or a whole river of clean water will not purify a pool unless you first clean the pool.

Just to say you are a Christian, and to talk about Christ's teachings in Sunday school is good, but not enough—you must clean out the well—put aside all bad language and cut out wrongdoing and then the Christian gospel will make you feel clean.

"*Cleanse first—within the cup, that the outside may be clean also.*"—MATTHEW 23:26.

To Remember

"Blessed are the pure in heart for they shall see God."

A PRAYER

Dear heavenly Father, we thank Thee for the beauty that is around us and for the ability to see Thy love working in the world.

Use us, O God, as young folks, that we may be good-natured and so give joy to our parents and to our neighbors, and be helpful, especially when our help is required.

Help us, when we see wrong being done, to try to stop it. Guide us always to be honest and trustworthy, that we may be dependable; and bless us all in Christ's name. Amen.

A Message from Our Bible

" One is your Master, even Christ.

But he that is greatest among you shall be your servant.

And whosoever shall exalt himself shall be abased; and he that shall humble himself shall be exalted.

Woe unto you, scribes and Pharisees, hypocrites! for ye make clean the outside of the cup, but within they are full of extortion and excess.

Thou blind Pharisee, cleanse first that which is within the cup that the outside may be clean also."—From Matthew 23.

KEYS

When your father starts the car he takes a key and inserts it in a little slot in the dash and turns it, steps on the starter or pushes the button and the engine starts.

Every lock has its own key,—indeed wherever there is a lock there is a key. When you come home and find the house door locked, I'll bet you know where the key is.

Then, too, you know about piano keys and organ keys —they have something to do with music. To have harmony you have to press down on the right keys.

Again if you had ever seen a log jam in a river as I have many times, you would see the river men looking for the one key log! Imagine just one little log causing thousands, yes millions to pile up and block the river so that nothing can float downstream!

Now, in the typewriting of the manuscript for this parable I saw a mistake: I struck an "i" for an "a" so that I had a "log jim" instead of a "log jam." The reason is that my mind works faster than my fingers! But if I want my readers to know I mean jam and not jim I must strike the right key on my typewriter.

So it is by your conduct, whether you are playing marbles or dolls or baseball, or in church or school, you are telling the world just what sort of boy or girl you are. Jesus teaches us to strike the right key for

---

"*—every man's works shall be made manifest.*"—I Corinthians 3:13.

To Remember

"Blessed are the peacemakers; for they shall be called the children of God."

A PRAYER

Dear God, we thank Thee for Jesus whom Thou didst send to us to teach us to live together in peace. Help us to be pleasant in disposition. Give us strength to turn aside from any desire to be angry and hateful.

Thy Son is our example by which we may govern our ways in speech and in deeds, as we work and play with our companions. Thou, O Lord, art the key to right living; may we always be near Thee, and, by using Thy love, radiate it through our lives. Bless our homes, we ask, and all our friends, dear Lord, and keep us clean and faithful in all our thoughts and ways. Amen.

A Message from Our Bible

"For other foundation can no man lay than that is laid, which is Jesus Christ.

Every man's work shall be made manifest; for the day shall declare it, because it shall be revealed by fire; and the fire shall try every man's work of what sort it is.

If any man's work abide which he hath built thereupon, he shall receive a reward.

Know ye not that ye are the temple of God, and that the spirit of God dwelleth in you?

If any man defile the temple of God, him shall God destroy; for the temple of God is holy, which temple ye are."—From I Corinthians 3.

33
THERMOSTAT

A THERMOSTAT is a gadget that has a long arm, so long that it reaches all the way from the little instrument on the wall of your living room down to the furnace in the cellar! Wouldn't it be nice to have a long arm like that so that you could reach the jam on the top shelf without dragging a chair into the pantry?

When the living room is cold the thermostat knows it and reaches a switch on the boiler and starts the heat coming in through the radiators; and then when it is warm enough it turns off the switch.

Have you ever been out in the woods and suddenly met a bear? I'll guess your hair seemed to stand right up on end, and your skin got cold. That's the way your nerves stretch out their arms and reach down into your heart and turn on more heat and energy, so that you can run faster or fight harder.

Have you boys and girls ever felt like crying? Perhaps you have been disappointed, or maybe you have been sad,—or just disgruntled and mad! It is then that you Christians reach up to God with the long arm of prayer and so God seems very close to you and you feel better right away. He puts new strength and hope and love into you so you forget, or overlook the thing that bothered you and you go cheerfully to work on something else.

"*Watch and pray.*"—MATTHEW 26:41.

To Remember

"Blessed are they which are persecuted for righteousness sake; for theirs is the kingdom of heaven."

A PERSONAL PRAYER

Dear God, reach into my heart and give me the power of restraint, for I am often tempted to dispute and argue and say cross words when I am asked to run errands or do some work. Thou art kind and will protect me while I sleep this night; lead me, tomorrow, to awaken happily, and to be thoughtful and helpful through the whole day.

Help me to make up my mind to be unselfish when others need my services. Keep me watchful for opportunities that I may be useful in bringing happiness to many who are less fortunate than I am. Bless them all, dear God, and this my home. Amen.

A Message from Our Bible

" Peter said unto him, Though I should die with thee, yet will I not deny thee. Likewise also said all the disciples.

Then cometh Jesus with them unto a place called Gethsemane, and saith unto the disciples, Sit ye here, while I go and pray yonder.

Watch and pray, that ye enter not into temptation; the spirit indeed is willing, but the flesh is weak."—From Matthew 26.

BELLS

Did you ever hear a carillon? A chime of bells, usually from a church tower? If you have ever heard such beautiful music from bells I'm sure you stopped and listened. Even though there was much noise in the street, the music of those bells came clear and sweet to your ears.

Another set of bells always attracts the attention of boys and girls.—When the clanging bell of the fire department comes ringing its warning down the street what a thrill it gives you,—and how you run to keep up so as to find out where the fire is!

When the doorbell rings you stop everything quickly and rush to see who is there. All other sounds are of little importance,—for someone has come to call. And when the telephone bell rings everyone who hears it is instantly alert. Someone turns off the radio; Sally stops playing the piano; Jimmy puts down his whistle; Brutus is made to keep quiet, and mother picks up the receiver and says "Hello" and then listens.

I cannot explain exactly to you what your conscience is —that quiet voice inside you that wants to tell you right from wrong, but I know this—when the question of right and wrong comes up you had better stop everything, for the bell of your conscience is ringing. So just stand still a minute, quietly, and take off the receiver and say—"Dear Lord, speak," and then listen.

"Behold I stand at the door and knock, if any man hear, I will come in."—Revelation 3:20.

To Remember

"Blessed are ye, when men shall revile you, and persecute you, and shall say all manner of evil against you falsely, for my sake."

A PRAYER

Dear Lord, keep us from jealousy and envy. Help us to be happy with what we have and grant to others the things that will bring joy to their lives.

We pray that we may have many opportunities to give some of our toys and books to those who are less fortunate than we are. Bless the children of other lands where war has brought sadness and distress; and make our country generous in helping them, and in teaching them Thy Christian gospel of faith and love, by our missionaries; in Christ's name we pray. Amen.

A Message from Our Bible

"As many as I love, I rebuke and chasten; be zealous therefore, and repent.

Behold I stand at the door, and knock; if any man hear my voice, and open the door, I will come in to him, and will sup with him, and he with me.

To him that overcometh will I grant to sit with me in my throne, even as I also overcame, and am set down with my Father in his throne."—From Revelation 3.

ROPES

Say, did you ever fall over a cliff and hang there in mid-air on the end of a rope? There you were with six hundred feet of nothing under you, waiting for someone to start pulling up on that rope. Then suddenly as you looked up at the rope above you, you saw one little strand break! You were pretty glad right then that someone pulled you up!

I have noticed that a rope doesn't just snap and come apart all at once. It breaks slowly. First a thread breaks, then a strand; and this weakens the other strands as it puts more weight on them so one by one they each start to break, until finally the whole rope is severed.

The steeple of our church was being shingled and I stood watching the men swing around on that high spire, just hanging to ropes! Every time a man pulled himself up to that dizzy height he examined the rope. He also told me he used a new rope whenever he went onto a new job.

A rope, to be strong, must have every thread, every strand whole, and bearing its part of the load.

Well, that's the way it is in the home and in the church or in your class. God wants and expects each member to do his part,—to be friendly, helpful, sharing and carrying his part of the load and helping each other build character.

"*Be strong in the Lord.*"—Ephesians 6:10.

To Remember

"Rejoice and be exceeding glad; for great is your reward in heaven."

A PRAYER

Give us Thy Christian strength, dear Lord, that, even though we may disagree with one another at times, we may not offend. Help us to realize that we live not just by, and for, ourselves; but all must be considered. So teach us to be thoughtful, and inspire us to do our part towards making the world one brotherhood.

Bless our church, O God, for by its teaching we all can live together happily as one family, working and playing together, finding the love of Jesus filling us with the desire to do Thy will that the whole world may live in peace.

A Message from Our Bible

" Finally, my brethren, be strong in the Lord, and in the power of his might.

Wherefore take unto you the whole armour of God, that ye may be able to withstand in the evil day, and having done all, to stand.

Stand, therefore, having your loins girt about with truth, and having on the breastplate of righteousness;

And your feet shod with the preparation of the gospel of peace.

Above all, taking the shield of faith, wherewith ye shall be able to quench all the fiery darts of the wicked."
—From Ephesians 6.

36

STENCILS

I WONDER if you all know what a stencil is. I will try to tell you. It is a thin piece of paper so made that when the typewriter letter hits it the letter is cut into the paper, and then the sheet is placed on a machine which holds ink and the ink runs through the letters that have been cut on the paper,—then you can read just what the stencil says. If a mistake is made on the stencil then that same mistake is recorded on every copy that is made. And so in the same manner if the stencil is cut perfectly right, then the copies we read are perfect.

A long time ago Jesus lived and grew up under God's direction, and so He came to be a Perfect Man. God then told Jesus to go about the world and stamp His life upon other people so that the world would gradually grow better because the people who were influenced by Jesus began to live like Him.

Did you ever see your mother make gems and salads in different shapes? Ask her about it sometime. I think you will find she poured the dough or the gelatin into moulds, and, when cooked or hardened, the contents came out the shape of the moulds.

Do the things you say and do remind others of the way of Jesus? Are you truly His friend so that you really try to do what He asks and be like Him?

"*Ye are my friends if ye do the things I command you.*"—JOHN 15:14.

To Remember

"Make a joyful noise unto the Lord, all ye lands."

A PRAYER

Dear Lord, we thank Thee for the church, through which Thy love may be stamped upon all nations of the earth.

Make us loyal, O God, and teach us to be friendly, that we may give joy wherever we are.

Bless the people in our country who speak a different language than we do, and help us all to know Thy gospel is for all races of men. We thank Thee, O God, for Jesus who taught us so much kindness and consideration; and may we, like Him, be willing to sacrifice, that Thy church may prosper in its great purpose. Use us in Thy name. Amen.

A Message from Our Bible

"If ye keep my commandments, ye shall abide in my love; even as I have kept my Father's commandments, and abide in his love.

This is my commandment, That ye love one another, as I have loved you.

Greater love hath no man than this, that a man lay down his life for his friends.

Ye are my friends, if ye do whatsoever I command you.

Henceforth I call you not servants; for the servant knoweth not what his lord doeth; but I have called you friends; for all things that I have heard of my Father I have made known unto you."—From John 15.

BENT TREES

I know where there are two beautiful birch trees bowing toward each other, in fact their tops touch and even overlap one another though they grow in the ground as much as twenty feet apart! My father once told me I was the cause of that! It seems that two of us boys, a long time ago, played in those trees and once we tied the tops together and left them. So you see they were bent because they grew that way.

Did you ever notice your grandfather's cane? I've seen many of those old canes all bent and crooked. It is probably some branch or tree root that grew that way.

I once saw a man whose back was so bent over that when he walked along the road his face was parallel to the ground. Due to some sickness he grew that way.

I like to see boys and girls with a lovely smile, showing teeth that are white and fairly straight, and that is the way most teeth are because somebody sees to it that they grow that way.

It also occurs to me that young folks need to watch their words and actions and thoughts so that they will grow straight, so that their soul will be upright and their conscience will let them look Jesus squarely in the face.

" The crooked shall become straight."—LUKE 3:5.

To Remember

"Serve the Lord with gladness; come before his presence with singing."

A PERSONAL PRAYER

I THANK Thee, dear God, for this beautiful morning. Help me to keep from doing anything I shouldn't today. As Thou hast protected me through the night, may I serve Thee during this day.

Make me fair when playing, and generous with the things I have, that others may be happy. May I be useful to someone today, that when night comes again I shall feel somewhat worthy of Thy protective care. Give Thy strength to each one of us in my home and direct our day for Thee, that by Thy guiding love we shall all grow to be more and more like Jesus. Amen.

A Message from Our Bible

" Prepare ye the way of the Lord, make his paths straight.

Every valley shall be filled, and every mountain and hill shall be brought low and the crooked shall be made straight, and the rough ways shall be made smooth;

And all flesh shall see the salvation of God.

Jesus also being baptized the heaven was opened,

And a voice came from heaven which said: Thou art my beloved Son; in thee I am well pleased."—From LUKE 3.

38

A BAG OF GRAIN

If you have never seen a threshing machine in operation, you've missed a lot of fun, also a lot of work; and perhaps you have missed losing a finger or even a hand in the machinery, for great rotating "beaters" grab the sheaf of oats which is pushed against them and pulls it into the separator and out comes the straw at one place and the nice heavy grain at the side.

The grain is put into bags holding about one hundred pounds, and after each half day's work I remember we all gathered around and carried those bags of grain to the bin which was about two hundred yards away, in another building.

I was a small boy when we used to do this on our farm and I learned a lot about life in those days,—I learned that when a man was talking he didn't try to shoulder one of those bags. He just waited and finished his story and then went to work! I also learned that the man who carried a bag of grain, holding it in front of him, made hard work of it and had to rest often. To drag it meant wearing out the bag and losing some of the grain. I couldn't manage some of those bags in either of those ways but, with a little help, I got a bag of grain on the top of my shoulder,—then I stood up straight and I could carry as many bags as any *man*.

You boys and girls will find you will have many "bags of grain" to lift,—things to do when you would much rather be skating. Don't drag them! Don't make hard work of them and fuss about it. Get *under* the load with determination and see how easy and pleasant it becomes.

"*Bear ye one another's burdens.*"—Galatians 6:2.

To Remember

"Know ye that the Lord he is God; it is he that hath made us, and not we ourselves; we are his people, and the sheep of his pasture."

A PRAYER

Dear Lord, we thank Thee for all Thou hast given us, —for a night's rest; for the day's opportunities. We thank Thee especially for the food prepared for our enjoyment, to give us strength and health for the work before us.

We pray for those who are hungry, that through our church we may generously give, so all may have enough, that their burdens of fear and want may be lightened. Help us to appreciate Thy great love that we too may express it, for Christ's sake. Amen.

A Message from Our Bible

"If a man be overtaken in a fault, ye which are spiritual, restore such a one in the spirit of meekness; considering thyself, lest thou also be tempted.

Bear ye one another's burdens, and so fulfil the law of Christ.

Be not deceived; God is not mocked; for whatsoever a man soweth, that shall he also reap.

For he that soweth to the flesh shall of the flesh reap corruption; but he that soweth to the spirit shall of the spirit reap life everlasting.

And let us not be weary in well doing."—From Galatians 6.

39
THE CLOCK HAD STOPPED

ONCE upon a time there was a clock that ticked! In order to make it go it had to be wound each day. One morning dad looked at that clock to see if it was time to get up,—and it was eleven o'clock! Well, dad knew it wasn't that late so he picked up the clock and found that it had stopped; so he gently rotated it expecting to hear it start ticking again; but no, it wouldn't go. Then he gently shook it, but even that did no good. Then he took it in both hands and gave it a hard shaking up and still it would not start ticking. Then he did what we all so often do, he started to take it apart and you know the rest,—it ended up at the clock store!

I had such a clock recently and I tried all those ways, except the last, to make it go and then in disgust I laid it face down on the mantel and what do you think, yes sir, it started ticking!

Quite often we meet people like that. Occasionally you and I are like that clock, we get discouraged, or disgruntled; sometimes downright mad and balky. We are so selfish we just stop working for God or the church; we don't feel like co-operating on a committee so we, too, stop. Friends, it's right then that we especially need to turn our faces down—bow our heads and pray God to help us, and He is sure to give us strength to start again.

"*Whatsoever ye shall ask in prayer, believing, ye shall receive.*"—MATTHEW 21:22.

To Remember

"Enter into his gates with thanksgiving and into his courts with praise; be thankful unto him and bless his name."

A PERSONAL PRAYER

Dear God, I thank Thee for strength and health,—for eyes that see clearly; for ears that hear plainly; for hands and feet for Thy service.

Help me care for them that I may see ways to be of use to people who need help and comfort. Let me hear only the good about people, and shut out all gossip and untruth.

Make me truly thankful, dear Lord, that I can impart to others, through my efforts, a sense of Thy great love and joy. Direct me in Thy name. Amen.

A Message from Our Bible

" Blessed is he that cometh in the name of the Lord; Hosanna in the highest.

This is Jesus the prophet of Nazareth of Galilee.

And Jesus went into the temple of God,

And said unto them, It is written, My house shall be called the house of prayer;

And all things, whatsoever ye shall ask in prayer, believing, ye shall receive."—From MATTHEW 21.

MASKS

Hallowe'en,—what an odd name. Most boys and girls like to have that day come because they can put on masks.

In ancient time it was a feast day in honor of all the saints. The druids or priests in charge of religious rites used to offer harvest gifts to their gods. These rites were usually done in an oak forest and bonfires were built and masks worn to frighten away the ghosts and evil spirits.

After a while people, even children, didn't believe in ghosts any more but the boys, and sometimes the girls too, loved to wear masks,—and I know you still do because at every Hallowe'en several come around and knock at my door and they look pretty scary. I expect it's a lot of fun to make believe scare someone, realizing no one will know who you are.

Sometimes people wear masks because they know the thing they are doing is wrong and they don't want to be known. Indians used to paint themselves to frighten off the white man and other tribesmen. I notice some girls also seem to have that same custom.

There are many, too many, people who wear masks that are not seen. A lie is a mask to cover up the truth of one's deeds. But God can see through it every time. We may sometimes fool people but we can never deceive God. Whatever we say or do, God knows exactly what we mean.

"Let no man deceive you with empty words."— Ephesians 5:6.

To Remember

"For the Lord is good; his mercy is everlasting; and his truth endureth to all generations."

A PRAYER

We thank Thee, dear Lord, for Thy teaching of the truth of life,—that love means joy and growth; that honesty brings happiness and peace; that sacrifice gives contentment.

We thank Thee that Thou didst give Thy life for all people, and as we read of distress and sorrow in the nations of the world, lead us to be generous and so give to them through our church, the medical and spiritual care they need. Thy example has taught us to love all races and nations, and to give them comfort and thankful hearts. Amen.

A Message from Our Bible

"Be ye therefore followers of God, as dear children;
And walk in love as Christ also hath loved us, and hath given himself for us an offering and a sacrifice to God;

Let no man deceive you with empty words; for because of these things cometh the wrath of God upon the children of disobedience.

Walk as children of light;

Proving what is acceptable unto the Lord."—From Ephesians 5.

41
STRAIGHT SWIMMING

For some reason all boys, and most girls, too, seem to like to go swimming. If the water isn't deep enough in the stream, bags will be found and filled with sand and placed across the brook to hold the water back and deepen the pool.

When swimming in a rather wide pool with the water rushing in all the time did you ever try to swim straight across? If, while swimming across, you watched the fishes and, perhaps, a bloodsucker or a turtle near by, you discovered that you didn't swim straight. Even if you walked across in that running water your tendency was to drift a bit downstream.

If you want to swim or walk straight across a stream of water fix your eyes on a boulder, or a tree or a house directly on the other side, then you will swim straight.

The same is true in walking on land or even in a room—if you look to one side, or close your eyes you will find it hard to walk straight. However, if you fix your eyes on a star, or the sun, or a distant hill or picture you can walk a straight course.

Walking through life is something like that. If you pay too much attention to things that are unimportant, just looking about and wondering if people are watching you, it won't be so easy to reach your goal. Fix your eyes and thoughts on God in the things you say and do, then you are better able to keep a straight course to your hopes and dreams.

"*—I believe in God.*"—Acts 27 : 25.

To Remember

"What doth the Lord require of thee, but to do justly, and to love kindness, and to walk humbly with thy God?"

A PERSONAL PRAYER

I KNOW, dear Lord, Thou hast made all things;
   I thank Thee for each one,
For Thy great love which ever brings
   New joys for days to come.

I thank Thee for my food today;
   For sleep that gives me rest,
For all my playmates wholesome, gay;
   For a home which Thou hast blest.   Amen.

A Message from Our Bible

"And now I exhort you to be of good cheer; for there shall be no loss of any man's life among you, but of the ship.

For there stood by me this night the angel of God, whose I am, and whom I serve.

Saying, Fear not, Paul; thou must be brought before Cæsar; and lo, God hath given thee all them that sail with thee.

Wherefore, sirs, be of good cheer; for I believe God, that it shall be even as it was told me."—From the story of Paul's shipwreck as told in ACTS 27.

42

ICEBERGS

Great hulks of ice keep breaking from glaciers when they reach the sea off the coast of Greenland and this floating ice is called an iceberg and it goes wandering around until it reaches warm water and finally melts. Some of these icebergs are hundreds of feet, perhaps almost a mile, across and a thousand feet deep.

If an iceberg looks big as we see it from a ship, we must remember that it is five or six times larger under the water,—hidden from our vision.

I am told they are very beautiful and upon occasion have saved the lives of fishermen who became stranded without water to drink, for of course the icebergs are formed from fresh water. So the iceberg is a friend.

Icebergs used to be dangerous to shipping and fishermen were afraid of them because they extended so far out under the water, and boats in the fog would hit them before the men realized they were near. But now there is little danger, as boats carry instruments which warn the lookout of their nearness.

How much like icebergs are people. Much of our lives is really hidden, in fact the really important things about us are not seen, such as courage, ambition, mental ability, pride, honor and, greatest of all, love. Even God we do not see, but He is in our hearts and by the instrument of prayer we can go to Him as a friend and find help.

"*We speak of God's wishes in a mystery even the wisdom that hath been hidden.*"—I Corinthians 2:7.

To Remember

"All things therefore whatsoever ye would that men should do unto you, even so do ye also unto them."

A PRAYER

We thank Thee, dear God, for the Bible which tells us so much of Thy plan for the world. Give us wisdom, we ask, that we may understand Thy great love for us, and make us worthy to receive it.

Give us courage to stand for those things that are right, even though some people may ridicule us.

Bless the children of other lands, and make us generous as we give for their comfort, in the name of Jesus. Amen.

A Message from Our Bible

"We speak wisdom among them that are perfect; yet not the wisdom of this world, nor of the princes of this world, that come to nought.

But we speak the wisdom of God in a mystery, even the hidden wisdom, which God ordained before the world unto our glory.

Which none of the princes of this world knew; for had they known it, they would not have crucified the Lord of glory."—From I Corinthians 2.

43
FILLING A BOTTLE

Did you ever try to refill one of those empty tooth paste tubes? or pour water into one of those play balloons?

I expect most of you have seen a Cape Cod barometer,—just a glass bottle with a kind of spout. When the water rises into that spout it's a sign that it may rain. I bought one once for a gift, and it took me nearly one hour to pour about two cups of water into it! I used a medicine dropper, I held it under the water faucet and I tried many ways, but more water went on the outside than in.

When you try to fill an ordinary bottle with water you have to pour it very slowly and tip the bottle at an angle else you will have nothing but bubbles,—and water all over the place.

It's not easy to fill a bottle with water, and the reason is very simple,—the bottle is full of air, and before you can get the water in, you have to drive the air out! I would think that a fortune would await the boy who could manufacture a bottle which would contain no air when empty, for a bottle full of air isn't of much use as it stands on the shelf.

There are a lot of things in your life at times that are of little use, and many things that should be driven out. Start filling your life right away with the love of God and the spirit of Jesus and all that is worthless will be driven out.

"*Be filled with the spirit.*"—Ephesians 5:18.

To Remember

"Teacher, which is the great commandment in the law? And he said unto him, Thou shalt love the Lord thy God with all thy heart, and with all thy soul, and with all thy mind. And the second, like unto it is this, Thou shalt love thy neighbour as thyself."

A PERSONAL PRAYER

I THANK Thee, dear Lord, that Thou art my Teacher. Help me to be a better pupil, that through my church I may learn more about Thy love and kindness and sacrifice.

Teach me each day to apply the lessons Thou hast taught me, that wherever I am, people will know, by my actions and words, that I am trying to be a true Christian.

Bless my home, dear God, and all who watch over me; and teach us all Thy way of living. Amen.

A Message from Our Bible

"See then that ye walk circumspectly, not as fools, but as wise.

Wherefore be ye not unwise, but understanding what the will of the Lord is.

Be filled with the spirit;

Speaking to yourselves in psalms and hymns and spiritual songs, singing and making melody in your heart to the Lord;

Giving thanks always for all things unto God and the Father in the name of our Lord Jesus Christ."—From EPHESIANS 5.

44
ROOTS SHAPE THE TREE

When I was a small lad, one day I noticed a tiny maple tree just starting to grow in the crevice of a large rock. It seemed such a strange place for a tree, so I would go and look at it about every week during that first summer. Then a few times each year I would go to that rock and sure enough the tree was still there and growing. But it grew rather misshapen at first, because, as I was told, the roots lacked depth.

I noticed the little branches were heavier on one side, because, as I could well see, they developed better; but after a year or two more, two of these branches died and the other side of the tree began to send out shoots. That was because the split rock now began to pinch the root on that side and the roots on the other side had just begun to get a fast hold into some soil.

Finally all the roots reached down below the rock and into rich loose soil and from then on until I had become a man that tree grew a normal, healthy, tall life on the top of that rock. One severe winter, however, it died. I suppose the exposed parts of the roots couldn't stand the intense cold of an extra hard winter. I miss that tree to this day. It worked so hard to grow I felt sad to have it die.

Just as roots shape the tree so the roots of character in your life shape your conduct. I certainly hope your character roots run deep into the fertile soil of God's love in order that your life and conduct may be strong and straight.

"*If the root be holy, so are the branches.*"—Romans 11:16.

To Remember

"Inasmuch as ye did it unto one of these my brethren, even these least, ye did it unto me."

A PERSONAL PRAYER

Dear Jesus, I thank Thee that Thou art a friend to all children. Help me to understand how, by helping folks who are in trouble or old, I am also serving Thee.

Keep me from jealousy, that I may better enjoy the things I have, and make me want to share them with others.

Bless the children of other nations who are sick and homeless, and use me to help them by my gifts through my church. May the pattern of Thy unselfishness be ever an example before me at home or at play. Amen.

A Message from Our Bible

"I beseech you therefore, brethren, by the mercies of God, that ye present your bodies a living sacrifice, holy, acceptable unto God, which is your reasonable service.

And be not conformed to this world; but be ye transformed by the renewing of your mind, that ye may prove what is that good, and acceptable, and perfect will of God.

For I say, through the grace given unto me, to every man that is among you, not to think of himself more highly than he ought to think; but to think soberly, according as God hath dealt to every man the measure of faith."—From Romans 12.

STAIRWAYS

When you want to pick cherries you put a ladder against the tree and climb up three, five, maybe seven or nine of those rounds until you come to the place where you can reach the branches loaded with fruit.

When you want to go to your playroom upstairs, how many steps do you climb,—don't look now, you have climbed them so often you ought to know, so guess,—now go and count them, are there thirteen or fourteen? If you stopped on the tenth stair you never would reach your room!

Stairways are made to lead to something higher up. Each step is very important, but it is not a landing, it is a means by which you *reach* a landing. Sometimes you like to play on the stairs, just run up and down, and that is a lot of fun but it doesn't get you anywhere.

I like that story about Jacob and his dream of a very long ladder which seemed to go up and up and up, and way up out of sight, even to heaven! How wonderful it would be to climb up stairs and see God! Well, Jesus came to show us how to do just that. Jesus is the stairway. Step by step, little by little, we come to know Him and so rise higher and higher toward God. Be sure, each day, by your conduct at home and at church or school, and especially at play, that you are stepping upward and coming nearer to pleasing God.

"*Behold a ladder was set up.*"—Genesis 28 : 12.

To Remember

"Not everyone that saith unto me, Lord, Lord, shall enter into the kingdom of heaven; but he that doeth the will of my Father who is in heaven."

A PERSONAL PRAYER

Dear Lord, teach me to be Thy servant and give me a greater desire to obey Thy will as my Master. In such partnership between us, Christianity will be strengthened in my town, and in the world.

Help me to be able to get along with other boys and girls. Don't let me be "bossy," but keep me ever thoughtful of the desires of others. Teach me not to expect to always have my own way! But make me humble that I may, step by step, climb nearer to the goal Thou hast set for me in manhood. Amen.

A Message from Our Bible

" And he (Jacob) dreamed; and behold a ladder set up on the earth, and the top of it reached to heaven; and behold, the angels of God ascending and descending on it.

And behold, God stood above it, and said, I am God.

And behold, I am with thee, and will keep thee whithersoever thou goest,—for I will not leave thee . . .

And Jacob awaked out of his sleep, and he said, Surely God is in this place,—this is none other than the house of God, and this is the gate of heaven."—From Genesis 28.

46
DOORWAYS

When you go into your house you enter through a doorway. At Christmas time your mother places a wreath on the door or upon the side of the doorway. She doesn't put it under a window or between windows, but in the doorway to make it look beautiful and to show a welcome to anyone coming to your house.

There is a book showing pictures of doorways and in it is one of a home I have entered many times, and the welcome in that home is as beautiful as the doorway indicates.

I am reminded at Christmas time about a famous doorway I have read about many times. Upon entering through the doorway of the Church of the Nativity in Bethlehem, a friend told me that one has to stoop else he would bump his head! Some say it is to make one bow as he enters this sacred shrine, but the true fact seems to be that years ago the Mohammedans did everything possible to annoy the Christians even to riding horseback into this church and leaving hoof prints on sacred places. In order to stop this the Christians walled up the doorway so that a person can only *walk* in and then by stooping!

If we are to preserve freedom and a Christian peace in the world there are many things we must wall out. Hatred and selfishness, intolerance and indifference, in our hearts must be kept out if we expect to welcome God's love, and make Christianity live through us.

"I had rather be a doorkeeper in the house of my God."—Psalm 84: 10.

To Remember

"If any man will come after me, let him deny himself, and take up his cross daily, and follow me."

A PRAYER

Thou art our Saviour, O Christ; lead us to follow Thee, that we may learn more of Thy love. Use us that we, who believe in Thee, may build a better world; a better town; a better home, as we work together in faith through our church.

Help us to know right from wrong, and to be faithful to Thee by our service and work in our church. We thank Thee for Christian leaders from whom we can learn right conduct.

Be with us in our play that we may be clean of speech and honest in decisions, and trustful of each other, being, ourselves, trustworthy. Amen.

A Message from Our Bible

" Blessed are they that dwell in thy house; they will be still praising thee.

Blessed is the man whose strength is in thee;

I had rather be a doorkeeper in the house of my God, than to dwell in the tents of wickedness.

For the Lord God is a sun and shield; the Lord will give grace and glory; no good thing will be withheld from them that walk uprightly.

O Lord of hosts, blessed is the man that trusteth in thee."—From Psalm 84.

A LEASH

Coughing, panting and with his tongue hanging out of his mouth a dog came struggling around the corner of the street! His collar was choking him pretty badly. So I could easily tell that he was dragging something with his leash, and sure enough he was,—yes, you are right—it was a boy.

Several weeks later I saw that same dog on a leash and he was still pulling on it, but this time it was backwards! The boy was trying to drag him into his house.

In both instances the small boy was mumbling to himself, and I could hear only a few words now and then; they were something like this: "wait" or "come along," "quit your pulling and you won't hurt yourself so much."

How right that boy was. It was the dog that did all the pulling causing the leash to be so tight. Each time the dog was pulling away from the boy who was trying to train him in the right way so he would be a gentle and gentleman dog, for a leash was not made to hang a dog with, or to hurt him but to lead and guide him.

Puppies are often like small boys and girls; they don't always know what the right thing is, so they pull on the leash, away from what they are told to do, until they learn how to be led, until they come to know that dad and mother always know best what is good for them. Just as boys want to make fine dogs out of puppies, so parents want their children to make fine Christian men and women. Let us also keep close to Jesus our Great Leader who will guide us to help make a better world.

"*For thy name's sake, lead me and guide me.*"— Psalm 31:3.

To Remember

"*Whatsoever things are true, whatsoever things are honourable, whatsoever things are just, whatsoever things are pure, whatsoever things are lovely, whatsoever things are of good report;—think on these things.*"

A PRAYER

DEAR God, teach us, for we want to know more about Thee. We want to know Thy will, and the way we should live. We want to know how to overcome feelings of dislike and jealousy.

We thank Thee for Jesus who has given us His example as a guide; and for His words of good advice.

Help us to feel that Christ is beside us urging us to do Thy will as a father who loves his children; for we know Thou art real,—even as love is real and powerful. So lead us, O God, as Jesus was led, in the way of truth and honor and justice, for His sake. Amen.

A Message from Our Bible

"In thee, O Lord, do I put my trust; let me never be ashamed; deliver me in thy righteousness.

Bow down thine ear to me; deliver me speedily; be thou my strong rock for a house of defense to save me.

For thou art my rock and my fortress; therefore for thy name's sake lead me, and guide me."—From PSALM 31.

ANVILS

PROBABLY not a boy or girl who reads this parable ever saw a blacksmith shoe a horse or an ox. If you have I wish you would write me and tell me about it.

After the old shoe has been pulled off and the nails removed the blacksmith prepares and shapes the hoof of the horse,—just like filing your fingernails. Then he takes down a brand-new piece of iron which is shaped something like a horseshoe and heats it red hot; then he picks it up with tongs and lays it on the anvil, a very heavy piece of iron secured to a block of wood, and pounds it with a heavy hammer until it begins to look as though it might fit the hoof. Then he plunges the hot iron into a tub of cold water which causes a volcano of steam to pour upwards to the top of the shop. When the shoe is cool enough he places it against the hoof of the horse just to try it and usually he has to heat it over again and pound it some more on the anvil. Without the anvil the blacksmith could not shape that new shoe which he finally nails on to the hoof.

You and I can do nothing without God. If you dislike someone just put yourself right next to Jesus and shape your thoughts the way He wants them.

If you have a temper or a mean disposition pound it out of you on the anvil of God's love. Put yourself right in Jesus' place. It's the only sure way to shape your life to the pattern of Christian character.

I find that the word " anvil " appears only once in the Bible and here it is:

"*—encouraged him that smote the anvil.*"—ISAIAH 41 : 7.

To Remember

"Finally, be strong in the Lord, and in the strength of his might."

A PRAYER

Our Father in heaven, encourage us with Thy hope. Give us strength to obey Thy will as given by Jesus.

We thank Thee for happy homes and cheerful friends, and we offer ourselves and our gifts that sadness and sickness may be relieved.

Bless the people in countries among whom so little is known of Thy great love, and use us as Thy helpers in giving Christianity to the world. Help us to be friendly and make us willing workers for Thee through Thy church, dear Lord. Amen.

A Message from Our Bible

"They helped everyone his neighbour; and everyone said to his brother, Be of good courage.

So the carpenter encouraged the goldsmith, and he that smootheth with the hammer him that smote the anvil, saying, It is ready for the soldering; and he fastened it with nails, that it should not be moved.

Fear thou not; for I am with thee, saith the Lord; be not dismayed; for I am thy God; I will strengthen thee; yea, I will help thee; yea, I will uphold thee with the right hand of my righteousness."—From ISAIAH 41.

WHAT COLOR IS A SNOWBALL?

WHAT'S the color of that snowball in your hand? "White" you say. Ah, look again! If I know a boy's hand after he has been playing outdoors for a few minutes, that snowball is not white! I ask again, what color is that snowball in an absolutely black-dark room? You probably think it is still white but how do you know? You can't see it! So it must be black, because everything in the room is black.

The beauty of color is as you see it under some kind of a light. If you look at that snow through a colored glass, then that snowball will be colored, to you at least. Some boys and girls are color blind. There are certain colors they can't tell from other colors.

You know I like to think of everything as being white until something comes between my eyes and any particular object. Why is a dress red? Because some red dye has come between one's eyes and some white cloth. Why does a white house sometimes look dark and dingy? Because it has been soiled by smoke and wind. I've seen a boy's white shirt come home from school that wasn't white at all! I guess you know why.

Did your mother ever say to you " O, but your face is dirty "? I don't mind at all seeing a boy with a dirty face, now and then, for I know he can wash it. But I am very sad when I see a boy or girl with a soiled tongue, or with hands soiled, not with dust, but with wrong deeds. Greediness, and the telling of wrong stories discolors the character of a boy or girl.

Keep yourself " unspotted from the world."—JAMES 1 : 27.

To Remember

"I am the bread of life; he that cometh to me shall never hunger; and he that believeth on me shall never thirst."

A PRAYER

Dear God, our Father, help us to think clearly, that we may learn more and more about Thy love; for only in that knowledge can we fully understand Thee and Thy purpose.

We thank Thee for Thy message as expressed and lived by Jesus, who kept Himself mentally and spiritually alert that physically He might be strong to resist wrong.

Use us, dear Lord, in Thy work through the church, the school or at play, and help us to be unselfish, and considerate of others as we would have them be toward us. Teach us, that we may know how to be good boys and girls. Amen.

A Message from Our Bible

"Let patience have its perfect work, that ye may be perfect and entire, wanting nothing.

But if any of you lacketh wisdom, let him ask of God who giveth to all liberally and upbraideth not; and it shall be given him.

But let him ask in faith, nothing doubting; for he that doubteth is like the surge of the sea driven by the wind and tossed.

For let not that man think that he shall receive anything of the Lord.

Pure religion before God is this, To visit the fatherless and the widows in their affliction, and to keep oneself unspotted from the world."—From James 1.

BRIDLES

I suppose you all know what a bridle is, but I doubt if many of you ever put one on a horse, to say nothing of a colt! Horses are used to being bridled. When they see you with one they hold the head down so that you can reach it, and open the mouth for the bits. In winter when the bits are very cold and frosty they will wait for you to blow on them, to warm them a little so that they won't stick to their wet lips.

I think a horse likes to be bridled because he seems to sense that it means he is to get out of his stall. It means exercise for him and it means safe guidance and service.

But a young colt doesn't know all this, so it rebels and what a time I have often had trying to convince a colt that a bridle won't hurt him. After a lot of patience, and trying, he finally learns that he cannot go out on the road without a bridle, so he submits.

I have a watch which keeps very good time. It is dependable because it is bridled. Before it was allowed to be sold to me as a good watch, men at the factory put some springs and wheels in it in such a way that the hands could go only just so fast. I also have a car, and I wouldn't go out in it unless I knew it had its bridles on. I like to think of its brakes and steering wheel as bridles.

The text I have for you today says something about keeping our mouth and tongue bridled, and when we are tempted to say or do something wrong just use that bridle of Christlikeness. Jesus will guide you right and give you complete happiness and freedom but also control.

"*I will sin not with my tongue, I will keep my mouth with a bridle . . .*"

To Remember

"I am the way, the truth, and the life; no man cometh unto the Father but by me."

A PERSONAL PRAYER

Dear Jesus, Thou Friend and Saviour, guide me every day, that I may always speak the truth. Grant that I may never hurt other people. Forgive me when I am cross and disagreeable at home, to those who love me and whom I love.

Help me to always think before I speak; and touch my heart and mind with the spirit of Thy great love.

Give me the needed strength that I may always have self-control in my talk and in my actions. Amen.

A Message from Our Bible

" I will instruct thee and teach thee in the way which thou shalt go; I will guide thee with mine eye.

Be ye not as the horse, or as the mule, which have no understanding; whose mouth must be held in with bit and bridle, lest they come near unto thee.

Be glad in the Lord, and rejoice, ye righteous; and shout for joy, all ye that are upright in heart.—From Psalm 32.

GOLD, FRANKINCENSE, MYRRH

Of course you know what gold is! Just a stone. Many, many years ago people used to pick up a bright looking stone and shine it by rubbing it with a piece of wool and wear it as an ornament about the neck or in the ears. Then, more civilized people came from other countries and saw these gold pieces of mineral and sold them for a great price, and because gold was so scarce it became very valuable and finally it came to be used as money.

Frankincense was the gum from an East Indian tree or the Norway Spruce I am told, and like gold it was hard to find and because of its scarcity it was very valuable and so used in the religious rites or sacrifices.

Myrrh was also a gum with medicinal properties taken from the bark of a shrub which grew in Abyssinia and Arabia, chiefly valued for its odor, and used, as was frankincense, as an offering in religious ceremonies.

When those religious Wise Men heard about Jesus being born in Bethlehem they considered Him to be a Great King who would have great power as a ruler so they brought gold in recognition of highest honor and the power that was to be in Jesus. And they also brought frankincense and myrrh because, being scarce, they were hard to obtain, and offered them as a valuable sacrifice, prophetic of the sacrificial life Jesus was to live.

The value in things is in their use! There isn't much fun in just looking at your doll or train! You want to know if it will talk,—if it will run! What good is a puppy if it won't play with you? Or a book if no one can read it? What about your words? your acts? If they aren't useful and helpful to someone please be careful what you say or do. Don't be common and cheap. Why do you give gifts? I hope it's because you want to. Because you love and respect your friends enough to sacrifice for them, and give something valuable, if it's only a kind word of praise, and your friendship.—MATT. 2: 11.

To Remember

"I am the Good Shepherd: the good shepherd giveth his life for the sheep."

A PERSONAL PRAYER

FATHER in heaven, Thou giver of all good things, hear my prayer as I worship Thee, and please consider our needs as a world.

I thank Thee for my home and the good times we have together here; but there are many homes that are not happy, many children who need things to make them comfortable.

Help me to see their need and to cheer these people wherever they may be,—in America or Africa; in Europe, in Asia or India.—Grant that they may have happiness too, even as my friends and I, who live in Christian homes, have it, for Thou did'st come to us as the giver of joy to all the world. Teach me to give my best to Thee. Amen.

A MESSAGE FROM OUR BIBLE

"When the Wise Men had heard the king, they departed; and lo, the star, which they saw in the east, went before them, till it came and stood over where the young child was.

When they saw the star they rejoiced with exceeding great joy.

And when they were come into the house, they saw the young child with Mary his mother, and fell down, and worshipped him; and when they had opened their treasures, they presented unto him gifts; gold, and frankincense and myrrh."—From MATTHEW 2.

CANDLES

Over three hundred years ago, when this country was being settled by our Pilgrim grandfathers there was no electricity. There were no beautiful electric lamps. Although there were crude oil lamps, candles were the most prominent in use. Today candles are used for decoration purposes and religious ceremonies.

I am informed that in Naples, back in 1924 it was thought to have a memorial to Enrico Caruso, that great tenor singer. So a great candle was built, the largest in history! It was eighteen feet tall and seven feet in circumference, weighing three tons, and every November second, All Souls' Day, it has been lighted and allowed to burn for twenty-four hours. It is estimated that this candle will last more than eighteen hundred years.

Nevertheless, the real use for candles or lamps is to give a light! You folks like to have fun, to dress up and go places. You like to play and have parties, but your main purpose is to serve God; to be useful and helpful, to be a real light in leading others to Christ. To stand up clean and straight and tall and point other boys and girls to Jesus' way of living. As long as there is one candle light, all is not dark, and as long as one boy or girl stands for the right, many will be drawn toward him and become other lights for God.

"*The candle is put on a stand that all they that enter in may see the light.*"—Luke 8:16.

To Remember

"I am the light of the world; he that followeth me shall not walk in darkness, but shall have the light of life."

A PRAYER

Our Father, we ask Thee to guide us through this day, that when night comes we may feel happy that we have been good boys and girls in our play. Help us do the work we have to do, without grumbling. Please give us clean hearts and right minds that our words may be truth, and our deeds unselfish.

Bless our homes,—our parents and brothers and sisters, and guide us to always speak pleasantly, and to act unselfishly. Teach us all Thy love, O God, and lead us in the way of Jesus. Amen.

A Message from Our Bible

"No man, when he hath lighted a candle, covereth it with a vessel, or putteth it under a bed; but setteth it on a candlestick, that they which enter in may see the light.

For nothing is secret, that shall not be made manifest; neither anything hid; that shall not be known and come abroad.

Take heed therefore how ye hear; for whosoever hath, to him shall be given and whosoever hath not, from him shall be taken even that which he seemeth to have."—From Luke 8.

53
CORRECT FOCUS

Did you ever try, with one ear, to listen to someone talk and with the other ear hear a dog bark? Or see a mountain peak with one eye and turn the other to look at a car go by? It's practically impossible,—you may hear and see both, but with both ears and both eyes!

It's like a magnifying glass, you hold it so that the sunlight will pass through it and as the rays strike one side, the glass pulls them together to focus them on a small object, and if that object is paper it will sometimes set it ablaze by these focused rays.

That is why some people wear glasses. They cause the vision of the eye as it passes through the lens to focus more quickly on the words of a book so that they will be more plainly seen.

Although a horse does not wear glasses, I am told that his eyes are so constructed as to focus his vision so that when he sees a man it makes him look very, very much bigger than he really is.

I think God wants you and me to be a kind of lens through which He may focus His love on the people of your town and bring them to become members of His Church. You all have ears to hear and eyes to see and hands to work with, and feet to run errands and a tongue to speak the truth. Focus your whole life, all you do or say, on Jesus Christ and you will be building a better world, by showing Him to people through your own conduct.

"*Now ye are the body of Christ and severally members thereof.*"—I Corinthians 12:27.

To Remember

"Come unto me, all ye that labour and are heavy laden, and I will give you rest."

A PERSONAL PRAYER

Dear Lord, teach me to pray. Guide my thoughts that they may not be scattered. Forgive me, when I pray, if my thoughts seem to stray to the ball game, or to the fun I shall have tomorrow. Let me think, these few minutes, just about Thee, and learn what Thou dost want of me.

Teach me to be loyal to the church, and dependable—so that people can trust me. Bless all young folks, dear Lord, and help us understand Thee and make us worthy of Thy love, by our talk and conduct, as we work and play together. Amen.

A Message from Our Bible

" For as the body is one, and hath many members, and all the members of that one body, being many, are one body; so also is Christ.

For the body is not one member, but many.

Now ye are the body of Christ, and severally members thereof."—I Corinthians 12.

DRILLS

Have you ever sat in the dentist's chair and have that buzzing drill massage the inside of a tooth? How soothing it feels, yes indeed! Doesn't it make you feel sleepy as you lay your head back and the drill starts humming its song?

Recently I read that eighty-five years ago Edwin Drake was sure there was oil deep down in the ground near where he lived in Pennsylvania, so, with a great drill he bored a deep hole in the earth and produced the first oil well in the world.

I saw a tree surgeon at work, not long ago. He was drilling into the tree and digging out the rotten wood to save the tree. So, there are many things that have to be drilled into, either to get rid of something bad or to produce something that is good.

So much is hidden beneath the earth's surface that has to be drilled for such as oil, gold, diamonds, coal, even clams and fishworms, but in order to be useful they must be brought to the surface.

Now, God knows that in your heart there is love and kindness and honor and truth and faithfulness and loyalty, all of which must be brought to the surface and applied before you are worth much. For instance, if you are an officer in your Sunday school class or young folks' organization I hope your loyalty leads you to every meeting even though it is sometimes hard to be there. The best drill I know is prayer. It will help you get rid of the wrong ideas and bring out the best that is in you.

"*This I pray that your love may abound.*"—Philippians 1:9.

To Remember

"Take my yoke upon you, and learn of me; for I am meek and lowly in heart; and ye shall find rest unto your souls."

A PRAYER

Dear Jesus, we thank Thee that Thou didst teach us to pray—for by talking to God we feel we are very near Him. Talking to Thee helps us to know the right path we should follow.

Keep us loyal to Thy church, dear Lord, and help us never to become lax in our service. Be very close to all young folks, that they may be used to spread Christian joy at home, or at school and always at play. Amen.

A Message from Our Bible

"I thank my God upon every remembrance of you.

Always in every prayer of mine for you all, making request with joy.

And this I pray, that your love may abound yet more and more in knowledge and in all judgment;

That ye may approve things that are excellent; that ye may be sincere and without offence till the day of Christ."
—From Philippians 1.

TIRE TREADS

I wonder if your father ever had an experience as I did not long ago, of skidding off the slippery road into a snowbank. I had to be pulled out. When I got home I looked at my tires and found that they were all pretty smooth.

Smooth tires cannot grip the road and they easily skid when the pavement is a bit wet, and to prevent such accidents it is well to keep the car on a straight path and have good treads on the tires.

I remember when I was a lad I put on a riverman's hobnail shoes, they were pretty big for me but I was anxious to see if I could stay on top of one of those logs. So I tried it, and I didn't! I got my feet wet and then some. But to the experienced riverman those nails in the soles of those shoes kept him from slipping off the logs,—of course he had to be well balanced too.

I notice that quite a lot of people wear creepers when they have to walk downtown on the slippery sidewalks. Creepers are just pieces of metal with treads on them, or rather sharp points that stick into the ice and keep one from skidding or falling down!

You know, God gives each one of us an opportunity to put treads on our lives! We can learn about Jesus and the love of God. We can learn how to be thoughtful and helpful and honest. Keep a good character and you will never slip on some cheap temptation to do wrong or to speak evil, for character is the tread in your life.

"Put on the armour of God that you may stand against evil."—EPHESIANS 6:11.

To Remember

" Thou wilt guide me with thy counsel."

A PERSONAL PRAYER

Dear Jesus, something happened today that I am sorry for; give me the strength of will to make it right before I lose the friendship of one of my chums.

Help me to control my temper; and keep my tongue from speaking evil words. Only Thy spirit of love and forgiveness in my heart can right such wrong and check me before I say thoughtless words.

Give me strength, dear Lord, and make me apply a Christian attitude at all times, that others may be led into Thy way.

A Message from Our Bible

" Put on the whole armour of God, that ye may be able to stand against the wiles of the devil.

For we wrestle not against flesh and blood, but against principalities, against powers, against the rulers of the darkness of this world, against spiritual wickedness in high places.

And take the helmet of salvation, and the sword of the spirit, which is the word of God;

Praying always with all prayer and supplication in the spirit . . ."—From Ephesians 6.

A BURNING COAL

No doubt most of your homes are heated by steam or hot water, and in order to produce steam or hot water in the radiators there must be very hot boiling water in the boiler downstairs and under the boiler there is a very hot fire. Some people use oil, and some use wood for fuel, but let us assume you are all using coal.

It would be pretty hard to start a good fire with one piece of coal, wouldn't it? Ask your father to try it for you some morning. It just can't be done. Even you would think it queer if you saw someone stoking the furnace fire by throwing in one little piece of coal at a time! In the first place it wouldn't give out any heat and in the second place the fire would soon go out.

Sometime go down to the cellar with your dad and look into that furnace. Notice that fine red-hot bed of coals; no wonder the steam sizzles in the radiators. Now reach in with the tongs and take out one single piece of coal and lay it on the ash barrel! How quickly it dies down, turns black and is soon cold. But if it's left in the boiler with the others it glows and burns and gives out heat for a long time.

Sometimes we think our nickel or even a dollar is not very big and can't do very much—well, that's the way with a piece of coal —— But let us take nickels and dimes and dollars and put them with what other people bring to church and together they send the power of God to all the world and our hearts will glow with love and satisfaction knowing we are helping other people with the warmth of Christianity, through the work of missionaries.

" *The Lord gives strength.*"—PSALM 29:11.

To Remember

"Thy word is a lamp unto my feet, and a light unto my path."

A PRAYER

We thank Thee, dear Lord, for the sun that brings warmth to the earth, and light to our path; beauty to the clear sky, and shadows.

Grant, O God, that we may so live and work with others in the church as to be guiding lights to people in need. Use us every day as we play, to show Thy spirit of fairness, that all may see clearly what is right and just in all decisions.

We thank Thee for Thy words in our Bible which teach us to know right from wrong. Help us to be obedient. Amen.

A Message from Our Bible

"Give unto the Lord, O ye mighty, give unto the Lord glory and strength.

Give unto the Lord the glory due unto his name; worship the Lord in the beauty of holiness.

The voice of the Lord is powerful; the voice of the Lord is full of majesty.

The Lord will give strength unto his people; the Lord will bless his people with peace."—From Psalm 29.

57

BRIDGES

Whenever we speak of bridges we usually think of a river or a small stream, and crossing from one bank to the other. Some bridges are over a mile long and made of heavy steel. Some are much shorter and made of wood. I love those covered bridges. When I was a boy, on my way to school every day I walked through one of the very longest covered bridges in New Hampshire at Bath, crossing the Ammonoosuc River; it's about four hundred feet long! When out fishing did you ever lay an old tree across the stream? That's a bridge too!

There is a bridge across the Atlantic Ocean. Think of that. It's a cable laid under the water over which words walk. I think the telephone wires and even the ether waves are bridges, for bridges are laid down to convey something from one point to another. That something usually is a person, a car, or a horse; but it may be also a conversation I should say.

I believe God wants us to be bridges over which He can travel into the hearts of others. Perhaps God has given you a great ideal, or some talent. He doesn't want you to be selfish and keep it for yourself, He wants you to pass it along to other people.

During a king's broadcast once, a wire broke, and so urgent and important was the message that a man picked up both ends of the wire and held on and so completed the circuit and the king's message passed through him to the public. So you boys and girls are bridges for God. He depends on you to get Jesus' message to people who need it.

"*Prepare ye the way of the Lord.*"—Isaiah 40:3.

To Remember

"Open thou mine eyes, that I may behold wondrous things out of thy law."

A PRAYER

Dear God, our Father, we thank Thee that Thy love works through us. Even though we are young we can be bridges, over which Thy kindness and joy may travel into other people's lives. Our parents are happier when we are good and not cross or fussy. Our chums like to play with us when we are not "bossy"!

Make us worthy and eager to help Thee, so that we can be useful in our church and loyal to our youth group, and that we may be found reliable when asked to do things by our minister and other leaders who work for Thee. Please bless our church, dear Lord, and our homes, and all who watch over us. Amen.

A Message from Our Bible

"The voice of one that crieth, Prepare ye in the wilderness the way of the Lord; make level in the desert a highway for our God.

And the glory of the Lord shall be revealed, and all flesh shall see it together; for the mouth of the Lord hath spoken it.

But they that wait for the Lord shall renew their strength; they shall mount up with wings as eagles; they shall run, and not be weary; they shall walk, and not faint."—From Isaiah 40.

ROADS—HAIRPIN TURNS

Several summers ago I traveled about nine thousand miles in our United States by automobile and you may be sure I saw all sorts of roads. There were many kinds I had never seen before, and in three of my parables I would like to describe three roads I shall long remember. This one is about hairpin turns.

Not very far away on the Mohawk Trail you ride along down the side of Hoosac Mountain when suddenly the road seems to end, so you slow down and actually stop, for ahead of you is a fence and a building, and beyond there is no road and no place to put one! The driver then will turn the car completely around heading back in the general direction from which you just came and you see the road continuing on down the mountain. Ask mother to show you a hairpin and you will see exactly the way that road looks, especially if you will bend the ends of that hairpin outward a bit.

So you follow the road and you will soon find yourself lower down the mountain and nearer your destination.

Most of you boys play football. When you want to carry the ball ten yards towards your goal you often have to run back in order to avoid the interference. We can't always go straight to where we want to go because it might upset other folk's plans; or run into trouble. I know Jesus would make many wide and hairpin turns if it meant going to help someone or to avoid hurting someone. If you saw a bear in your path on your way home you would quickly make a hairpin turn and go home some other and safe way! So when you catch yourself wanting to say something mean, make a hairpin turn and proceed by way of pleasant words.

"Let the words of my mouth—be acceptable unto thee . . ."—Psalm 19:14.

To Remember

" Thy word is truth."

A PRAYER

Dear God, we know Thy way is truth. Help us to follow in Thy footsteps, and keep us from choosing a wrong road lest we come to a " dead end." Bless them who teach us in church and at home, and make us think before we allow thoughtless boys and girls to lead us into wrong lanes.

By Thy patient leadership, dear Lord, use us as Thy scouts to follow Thy way of love and service, that many young folks may come to accept Thee as their Master.

A Message from Our Bible

"—cleanse thou me from secret faults.

Keep back thy servant also from presumptuous sins; let them not have dominion over me; then shall I be upright,

Let the words of my mouth, and the meditation of my heart, O Lord, be acceptable in Thy sight, O Lord, my strength, and my redeemer."—From Psalm 19.

ROADS—SWITCHBACK

Out in the Big Horn Mountains of Wyoming several summers ago, I lifted the car I was driving to an altitude of nearly ten thousand feet. That is nearly two miles right up into the air, almost twice as high as Mount Washington in New Hampshire.

In order to get to the top we had to zigzag our way back and forth on what is known as a switch-back road. The best illustration I can think of to describe this road is an ant climbing a ladder, using all the rounds! He starts up the side pole, walks across the first round, climbs the other side pole and walks across the second round and so on to the top—a switch-back road. Each crossing of the rounds brings him a little higher. So we would drive along about one mile and make a hairpin turn and drive in the opposite direction one mile and then do it all over again, but each new level brought us about three hundred feet higher up the mountain. We could look down on the road on the lower level and talk to those coming up!

It was rather dangerous and many people have been killed each year by running off the road and falling over the precipice two thousand feet below. We had to drive twenty-one miles to reach the top of that mile and a half hill. But it was worth it. The view was beautiful and glorious, and we threw snowballs in August! But it did take a lot of patience to reach the top. Indeed, a lot of things are done better with patience. I used to have to pick up potatoes and sometimes a rotten one was thrown in among the good ones, and then in a few weeks others began to rot. I should have been in less of a hurry. More patience would have saved a lot of trouble. Paul tells us to do our work well even though it takes a bit longer.

"*Run with patience the race set before us.*"—Hebrews 12:1.

To Remember

"Blessed is the man that walketh not in the counsel of the ungodly, nor standeth in the way of sinners, nor sitteth in the seat of the scornful."

A PERSONAL PRAYER

Dear God, our heavenly Father, forgive me when I am impatient with words. I know I speak too quickly sometimes and say things I should not say.

Help me to realize that I am not always right, and that I can learn a great deal by listening to the advice of older people.

Bless my home, dear Lord, and grant that I may be worthy of the trust that my parents have in me. Use me in spreading the truth of Thy love that all who are indifferent may possess Thy blessing. Amen.

A Message from Our Bible

"Whatsoever things were written aforetime were written for our learning, that we through patience and comfort of the Scriptures might have hope.

Now the God of patience and consolation grant you to be likeminded one toward another according to Christ Jesus;

That ye may with one mind and one mouth glorify God, even the Father of our Lord Jesus Christ."—From Romans 15.

ROADS — PIG-TAIL

Away out in South Dakota there are some very steep mountains known as the "Black Hills." On one of those "hills" designated as Rushmore, a man has chiseled out the faces of several of our United States presidents. Of course I wanted to see this great work which the sculptor had done, so I had to drive to the top of Iron Mountain just opposite Rushmore. Believe me, the road was the crookedest and the craziest I have ever seen. You just can't believe it until you see it, and I certainly hope all of you will some day.

Did you ever see the tail of a live pig? It's almost as curly as the spring that holds your bird cage! Well, the road up Iron Mountain was something like that! Twice I drove the car over a bridge under a bridge and up over that bridge over the one I had just crossed and under another, and then up over the third bridge above the second bridge. Now, that's perfectly clear, isn't it! Ask your father or big brother to explain it to you! But you really have to see it to believe it.

It certainly was worth the climb to look across a narrow gorge onto Rushmore Mountain and see the faces of Washington, Jefferson and Lincoln—and now one more is in evidence, that of Theodore Roosevelt.

As I thought of that pig-tail road which lifted us to a higher altitude but didn't seem to get us much nearer our destination for a time, I thought of you boys and girls studying, and going to church school learning about Jesus. Progress seems to be slow and you don't feel that you are getting ahead very fast,—but you are; you are all the time being lifted just a bit higher until one day you will realize the beauty of God's love if you but patiently do His will day by day.

"*Study to show yourself approved unto God.*"—
II Timothy 2:15.

To Remember

"His delight is in the law of the Lord; and in his law doth he meditate day and night."

A PRAYER

We thank Thee, dear Father, for our Christian homes; and for the churches whose ministers and missionaries are preaching the gospel of Jesus, leading our country and the world to higher standards of thought and character.

Show us the way, dear God, and help us learn how, by our own consecration and reverence, and patience, we can, as we grow older, be an example of right living by studying Thy will and obeying Thy commands.

Help us to be faithful and to never leave that Christian road of life over which Jesus traveled and taught us to walk in. Amen.

A Message from Our Bible

" Thou therefore, my son, be strong in the grace that is in Christ Jesus.

Study to show thyself approved unto God, a workman that needeth not to be ashamed, rightly dividing the word of truth.

But shun profane and vain babblings; for they will increase unto more ungodliness.

—Let every one that nameth the name of Christ depart from iniquity."—From II Timothy 2.

SALT

Jesus, evidently, thought that salt was one of the most important things to physical life so I think it will be interesting to suggest to you some of the known facts about salt and its value.

Salt not only makes things taste better but you would die without it! I am told there are some tribes who live on raw meat. They never eat salt because they don't need to—you see the salt is in the raw meat of the animal they eat. When meat is cooked this salt is lost and it needs to be salted.

Salt preserves your cucumbers. It even "freezes" your ice cream! It is one of the essential things TO life and IN life.

In some places salt is very scarce, and it was once used for money. The ocean water is a little less than three per cent salt. The Great Salt Lake is twelve per cent salt. It's a spectacular and beautiful sight to see those salt flats in Utah, like snow, covering the ground.

The largest salt mine is probably in Poland where a whole village under ground is built of salt.

Here is an interesting fact someone has worked out: the salt from all the waters of all the seas in the world amounts to about four million, five hundred thousand cubic miles, or enough to cover the whole earth with a layer of salt one hundred twelve feet thick!

You see God made salt plentiful, because it is so essential. God wants Christians to be more plentiful too, because the teachings of Jesus are essential in making the world better, in making your town or city a better place to live in. Christianity preserves the best things and destroys the evil and the wrong, just as salt will kill poison ivy and destroy termites. Indeed Jesus said of Christians:

"*Ye are the SALT of the earth.*"—Matthew 5:13.

To Remember

"He shall be like a tree planted by the rivers of water, that bringeth forth his fruit in his season; his leaf also shall not wither; and whatsoever he doeth shall prosper."

A PRAYER

Dear Lord, we thank Thee for our food and for health to enjoy it. Bless those who work hard to prepare it for our use. As it makes us strong physically, may Thy love make us strong of character.

Teach us the way of Jesus, O God, that Christianity may, by our efforts, be accepted by all people of the earth, to sweeten life and preserve peace among men and nations. Help us to learn from Thy life, dear Lord, how to grow unselfishly and without envy or jealousy, and to be thoughtful of others' needs. Amen.

A Message from Our Bible

"Ye are the salt of the earth; but if the salt have lost his savour, wherewith shall it be salted? It is thenceforth good for nothing, but to be cast out, and to be trodden under foot of man.

Ye are the light of the world. A city that is set on a hill cannot be hid.

Let your light so shine before men, that they may see your good works, and glorify your Father which is in heaven."—From Matthew 5.

GLASS HOUSES

SOMEONE once said, "He who lives in a glass house should not throw stones." Do you think you would like to live in a glass house even if you didn't want to throw stones?

I once heard of a man who did live in a glass house! It was said to be beautiful. It glistened in the sun. But it was surrounded by a high board fence so very few ever saw it while the man who lived in it was alive. He was a very rich man and a very selfish one. He had no friends and wanted none apparently. No one ever entered that glass house, until the owner died and then people discovered something!

It was a glass house, but every sheet of glass was a mirror inside. The rich man who lived in it could not see out—he could, and desired only to see himself.

Your first thought is that no one could be so utterly silly and selfish, yet I have seen many houses with high fences around them so that their beauty and elegance cannot be enjoyed by others. There are, unfortunately, many people like that. They make no friends because they are not friendly. Like Scrooge, they just live for themselves.

That is not much like Jesus, is it? How friendly He was to children as well as to grown-ups. How He loved to sacrifice for them and help them. He truly lived the words He once said for our guidance:

"*Thou shalt love thy neighbour as thyself.*"—LUKE 10:27.

To Remember

"*The ungodly . . . are like the chaff which the wind driveth away. Therefore the ungodly shall not stand in the judgment, nor sinners in the congregation of the righteous.*"

A PERSONAL PRAYER

Dear Jesus, I thank Thee for the many examples of Thy great love for children. Teach me to be friendly towards people whose ways I do not like. Keep me from agreeing with their wrong ways and thoughtless words, and make me strong that I may help them by my own actions.

Restrain me, O God, from saying things that hurt, and grant that I may always show that I am a Christian.

Bless our church, and make me worthy of Thy trust in me that Thy friendly spirit may be shown in my attitude when working or playing.

A Message from Our Bible

" And behold, a certain lawyer stood up, and tempted him, saying, Master, what shall I do to inherit eternal life?

He said unto him, What is written in the law? how readest thou?

And he answering said, Thou shalt love the Lord thy God with all thy heart, and with all thy soul, and with all thy strength, and with all thy mind; and thy neighbour as thyself.

And he said unto him, Thou hast answered right; this do, and thou shalt live."—From Luke 10.

63
THERMOMETERS

I HAVE a thermometer outside my window so that I can tell how cold it is on a winter's morning without going outdoors. I have seen the mercury in that thermometer as low as fifty below zero!

Sometimes when you are sick the doctor comes and puts a thermometer into your mouth. He sees that your temperature is 101 so he comes again the next day until it registers 98.6, then he knows you are normal and well again.

One day a flock of measle germs come your way and make you a visit and start to work on you. Then your blood begins to over-heat your body IN ORDER TO KILL THOSE GERMS. You say you are sick because you have a fever and the thermometer registers 103. The real fact is, you have a fever because you are sick. That fever is working for you—it's your best friend, for it kills those germs. You see that is the way God takes care of you. But of course you must do your part and help that fever in its work. You must also take care of your body by eating the right things and getting plenty of sleep, because germs cannot break down healthy bodies, and then your temperature will stay at the normal place where God intended it to be and so grow strong and happy, anxious to work hard for God who has done so much for you.

I never read of Jesus being sick. He was so strong and athletic. He never allowed anything to harm His body. He shunned any bad habits as He would scarlet fever germs, so it was said of Him,—

"*The child grew and waxed strong.*"—LUKE 1:80.

To Remember

"For the Lord knoweth the way of the righteous; but the way of the ungodly shall perish."

A PRAYER

FATHER in heaven, as Thou hast loved us, grant that we may find the way to love each other. Even when we feel we are talked about, help us to make things right; and keep us from angry words and hateful deeds, that we may be calm in attitude.

Give us the strength, as Jesus showed, to overcome unkind thoughts and to help those who are weak and indifferent to the Christian character that all, under Thy loving care, may become more and more like Him. Amen.

A Message from Our Bible

"And thou, child, shalt be called the prophet of the Highest; for thou shalt go before the face of the Lord to prepare his ways;

To give knowledge of salvation unto his people by the remission of their sins.

Through the tender mercy of our God—

To give light to them that sit in darkness—to guide our feet into the way of peace.

And the child grew, and waxed strong in spirit, and was in the deserts till the day of his shewing unto Israel."
—From LUKE I.

INSULATORS

I READ a sad, sad story some weeks ago in the daily paper of an innocent looking, bright copper wire dangling from a pole. It was pretty so a small child grabbed it with its chubby hands and was terribly burned. Men who work with those wires and know how to handle them have no trouble—they wear a certain kind of gloves. These gloves are insulators. The live electric power rushing through those wires doesn't seem to like the looks of these rubber insulators so passes right along without jumping off.

Why do you suppose those little glass cups are placed up there on those poles with the wires attached to them? They are insulators, or non-conductors, put there so that the current of electricity will not be side-tracked and hop down the pole. These insulators are something like a right-of-way switch on a railroad track. The train goes right through safely to its destination, but if someone had turned the switch or broken it there might have been a wreck, and many would have been hurt.

So, without the glass insulator the electric current, rushing through those wires, might, in a rain, be switched down the pole to the harm of someone leaning against it.

I like to see boys and girls, and older people too, who are well insulated! Whose loyalty to God and to a great Christian purpose never "jumps the track," who never allow anything to interfere with their doing the right thing, who never seem to get tired, and so jump off the "wire" that takes them to their goal; or greedy, and try to make "short-cuts."

Insulate yourself with the love of Jesus and carry through with God's message.

"*When thy eye is single, thy whole body is full of light.*"—LUKE 11:34.

[127]

To Remember

"The heavens declare the glory of God; and the firmament sheweth his handywork."

A PRAYER

Dear God, we are thankful that Jesus grew up in a home whose parents, like ours, loved Him; who taught Him to work and never to shirk.

Through Him Thou could speak to the people of this world and show us, by His experience, how to live. Teach us to be straightforward and honorable in all we do. Keep us loyal to the highest ideals and help us declare Thy message of love and peace by our attitude, and to see clearly Thy will when at play or work.

We thank Thee for the very joy of living,—help us make the most of it by being loyal and useful in our homes and in Thy church. Hear our prayer, O Lord, and guide our steps aright. Amen.

A Message from Our Bible

"No man, when he hath lighted a candle, putteth it in a secret place, neither under a bushel, but on a candlestick, that they which come in may see the light.

The light of the body is the eye; therefore when thine eye is single, thy whole body also is full of light; but when thine eye is evil, thy body also is full of darkness.

If thy whole body therefore is full of light, having no part dark, the whole shall be full of light, as when the bright shining of a candle doth give thee light."—From Luke 11.

COINS

I BROUGHT out my box of old coins some time ago and in looking them over I wondered how much some of them might be worth. I sent several of the best ones to a man who would know and he told me that they were worth nothing. They were worn too much, so they were of no special value because no one would want them. I doubt if they were worth their face value because one could not read the printed matter on them.

Coins, to be good as money, must be used and good enough to be kept in circulation and especially they must bear the stamp of a recognized government. If the name of the government cannot be read on the coin it is taken out of circulation and melted over and new coins are minted.

A dollar bill isn't worth the paper it's written on unless the true stamp of the United States is on, and if there should be anything wrong stamped on it that whole issue of bills is quickly called back, for their value is gone.

Whether a coin is a penny, a nickel or half dollar or a "cartwheel" silver dollar, its true value is what the government says it is.

That's the way it is with you and me, our value is what God rates us. Friendship, like money, grows more valuable by use,—by circulation, and if we live selfishly we will soon find that God's stamp of approval will not be visible upon us and so we just won't be very valuable.

A coin, then, to be worth its face value must be loyal to the government it represents. Let us proudly show the world that loyalty to God is stamped upon us, is plainly seen by all and then our value to our community, our church and to God is very great.

"*Ye are my friends, if ye do the things which I command you.*"—JOHN 15: 14.

To Remember

"*The law of the Lord is perfect, converting the soul; the testimony of the Lord is sure, making wise the simple. The statutes of the Lord are right, rejoicing the heart; the commandment of the Lord is pure, enlightening the eyes.*"

A PERSONAL PRAYER

I thank Thee, dear God, for all the friends I have, to play with and to work beside. Teach me to be thoughtful and friendly in all I do and say.

I thank Thee too, for Queenie, and all animals and birds that give young folks so much pleasure in their homes and in the fields.

They are such loyal friends, please grant that we may always be kind to them and never neglect them in winter and in storms when they need protecting care.

Help me always to be obedient to the wishes of my father and mother for they know best what is good and right, and by them I shall know Thy will better. So lead me to express my faithfulness to Thee by my loyalty to my home and church. Make me Thy true friend. Amen.

A Message from Our Bible

"Ye are my friends, if ye do whatsoever I command you.

Henceforth I call you not servants; for the servant knoweth not what his lord doeth; but I have called you friends; for all things that I have heard of my Father I have made known unto you.

These things I command you, that ye love one another."—From John 15.

PICTURE FRAMES

Have you a camera? If so, did you ever say about some picture you had taken: "That's good enough to frame?" So you go frame hunting and you try several before you finally find the one you like for that particular picture.

A frame sets off a picture. It can sometimes cause the picture to seem even more beautiful than it is, but usually it just brings out its beauty. If it's a photograph it sort of makes it LIVE.

Then too a frame protects the picture, with the glass in front, it keeps grit from getting onto it. It also keeps the picture in shape so that it doesn't fold and wrinkle; and it keeps it right side up.

Always remember this, boys and girls—God created life in this world and set it in the frame of *you,* and He expects you to give strength and loveliness to that life by taking very good care of yourself, the frame. Whenever a picture frame looks shabby people look at the frame and say, "That might be a nice picture if the frame didn't spoil it."

So it is when I see a girl or boy sit down to dinner with unclean hands and fingernails I just wonder what the matter is. Something is wrong inside, with the ideals or character or training of that child. It may not be the child's fault but it does reflect on him just the same. Clean body and teeth and tongue go far to show what is inside a boy's heart. Or a child's home!

God gave you the frame of your body, and the way you take care of it, and respect it, shows up to the world what your life really is.

"*For life is more than meat.*"—Luke 12 : 23.

To Remember

"Let the words of my mouth, and the meditation of my heart, be acceptable in thy sight, O Lord, my strength, and my redeemer."

A PRAYER

Our Father in heaven, help us to realize the importance of keeping clean and strong, physically, mentally and spiritually; for our great purpose in life is to be more and more like Jesus in thought and attitude.

Give us the strength to develop a right character, that whatever we say or think may be pleasing to Thee. So help us to overcome jealousy and hate in our hearts, lest we express them in our actions. Give us the feeling of love that it may show in the brightness of our face, and in our obedience to Thy will as taught us in our home and in our church.

Accept our prayer, dear Lord, as evidence that we truly trust Thee, and desire to serve Thee, that Jesus' way may, through us, come to be the way of mankind in peace and in love. Amen.

A Message from Our Bible

"And seek not ye what ye shall eat, or what ye shall drink, neither be ye of doubtful mind.

For all these things do the nations of the world seek after; and your Father knoweth that ye have need of these things.

But rather seek ye the kingdom of God; and all these things shall be added unto you."—From Luke 12.